ARTHUR CLUES
SAINT AND SINNER

MAURICE BAMFORD

Maurice Bamford

VERTICAL EDITIONS

www.verticaleditions.com

First published in the United Kingdom in 2008 by
Vertical Editions, 7 Bell Busk, Skipton,
North Yorkshire BD23 4DT

www.verticaleditions.com

ISBN 978-1-904091-26-4

Cover design and typeset by HBA, York

Printed and bound by the Cromwell Press, Trowbridge

CONTENTS

ACKNOWLEDGEMENTS

Writing the biography of the outstanding hero of my childhood was an adventure I could not have completed without the help of a number of people both here in Great Britain and in that wonderful country, Australia. Guidance in researching Arthur Clues' youthful career in all three of his sporting activities: rugby league, rugby union and cricket, was given wholeheartedly by some well respected Australian Journalists: Sean Fagan, Ian Heads and Geoff Armstrong. Sean Fagan was also instrumental in guiding me towards a superb group of archivists dedicated to keeping the memory of the Western Suburbs Magpies rugby league club alive. Ben Fisher, Ray Bernasconi and Craig Woodley were my contacts at the Magpies Archive and they supplied me with some great copy. A good friend of mine in Australia, Richard Fenn, researched Arthur's younger days out in Parramatta.

Arthur's former team mates, Ted Verrenkamp, Cliff Last and Geoff Gunney MBE, helped me tremendously with their memories of his deeds. Leeds Rhinos club president, Harry Jepson OBE filled in lots of spaces in the big man's career, as did ex Leeds RLFC secretary Bill Carter and current Rhinos match time keeper Bill Watts. A huge amount of facts and figures were very kindly supplied by rugby league historians Robert Gate and Ray Fletcher (who also kindly wrote the foreword) while Leeds historian, Phil Caplan, was on hand to help with additional bits and pieces. The Rugby League Journal's Harry Edgar, the 'son of the Cumbrian soil', helped me considerably with facts and photos and former Barrow player, the late great Jim Lewthwaite, contributed further key information.

To all who helped me in this work to remember a great player and a true character, I say a big thank you. A final thanks must go to Mrs Muriel Clues for supporting me in writing this book about her late husband and for providing a true insight into 'Big Arthur's' character.

FOREWORD

'Call that a Test match? Rubbish! Nobody got hit.' That was Arthur Clues' usual reaction whenever I enthused over a brilliant clash between Great Britain and Australia. We were living in different worlds, of course. He longed for the ferocious clashes of the forties and fifties when Test matches were often tagged with war-time titles: 'The Battle of Brisbane', 'The Battle of Odsal…' I cringed at some of those clashes and delighted in the more disciplined games of later years.

He was too polite to say so, but I think he regarded me as a softy. Arthur loved to talk about the 'biff' and would roar with laughter even when the punch (literally) line had him flat on his back. He always got his own back, you see. Even listening to his stories made me apprehensive, because his intended friendly slap on the back was delivered with the force of a crunching tackle.

So was he a monster? Far from it. 'Big 'arted Arthur' summed him up perfectly. But even on the field there was much more to him than the uncompromising enforcer image he liked to embellish. For a big man he was extremely nimble on his feet, with a side step here and a swerve there. His ball distribution was also equal to that of a half-back and these days he would have handled the much smaller ball like a pill in his shovel-sized hands.

As a young Hull supporter in the 1950s, I thought Bill Drake and Harry Markham were the perfect second row partnership; Arthur Clues was the pair combined. He had the skills of Drake and the hard, straight running of Markham. In fact, you could throw in the aggression (and that's a euphemism) of mighty prop Jim Drake to complete Arthur's ranking as one of the all-time great forwards.

But comparisons of players from different eras are good only for bar room discussions. The game has changed so much over the years. Yet Arthur Clues had such a range of skills and intimidating power that he would have been good in any era. I doubt, however, if he would ever have been a super sub. His impact began at the kick off and he would not have taken kindly to being brought off after his 10 or 20 minutes were up. What a relief that would have been to the opposition.

In getting Maurice Bamford to write this book on one of his heroes the publishers have made a shrewd choice. It is not a work of literature, but it is full of passion and admiration for a player whose career deserves to be recorded for posterity.

Raymond Fletcher
Yorkshire Post Rugby League Correspondent 1975-1995

INTRODUCTION

Arthur Clues is often accepted as the best ever second row forward in rugby league football. Because he was a larger than life character who spoke using superlatives that would have made a chief stoker blush, it is not surprising that descriptions of Arthur Clues' deeds on and off the field occasionally seem mythological. So many tales about the great man verge on the unbelievable that those hearing them for the first time often disbelieve them.

A likeable factor about 'Big Arthur' was his rich and strong Australian accent, highlighted and punctuated in his conversation, especially when he let his hair down, by the use of rough and often x-rated language. The nickname 'Big Arthur' was self explanatory. He was a big man. He stood 6 foot 1 inch tall and performed in his playing career at his best when he was around 15 and a half stone. He played very much bigger than that. His physique for a back rower was magnificent. In Arthur's heyday not many forwards possessed the three-quarters type skills in general attacking play. The forwards were tacklers, drivers in of the ball when clearing their own line and labourers to the three-quarters tradesmen. But big Arthur changed all that. He had natural pace and was exceptionally quick for a big man. He ran, when breaking clear, like an international centre and could blitz through the tightest defence with power and sell dummies to slice through with the dexterity of a stand off half. He possessed the sweetest little side step ever seen, more like a gentle prop off either foot and bang, he was striding through the gap. His sheer size and pace on the run allowed him to fire that steam hammer hand-off that could have demolished a block of flats. And his ultra accurate left foot produced long, raking touch finders of 30, 40 and even 50 yards. His other forte was the chip over the advancing defensive line. This he did with unerring accuracy. He would run at the line, then as they hesitated he chipped the ball over them, raced after it and with superb success rate, retrieved the ball on its first bounce (it always seemed to bounce back towards him), then away he ran, usually clear to the full back. His overall kicking game was tremendous, he rarely lost possession either going for touch or chipping for himself.

Arthur's defence was brutal. He was a 'hurting' tackler. He was of the old school who preached that tackling around the legs hurt nothing except the tackled players' feelings. His target area was across the chest, or most times just about nine inches higher! His total focus on winning and gaining winning money made him the most intimidating competitor, because he would, if necessary, trample over an opponent to gain an advantage, which was not unusual in those days.

In the 1940s and 1950s certain things that went on during a game would not be tolerated today because of the clean up of foul play in recent years. Dust ups and toe-to-toe fighting was fairly commonplace then. This wouldn't happen every 10 minutes of course but it was certainly commonplace. Very few forwards embraced the Corinthian spirit in those days. Arthur's tough outlook alone did not make him stand out above the rest. Most top forwards would stand on any player's face to win and never bat an eyelid. In my humble opinion, Arthur Clues was the best second rower I ever saw, an opinion I share with many of his former team mates and opponents. Some of the greatest accolades ever given to an overseas player in this country have been repeated over and over by great players who crossed swords with him. In each case it was said, 'He could give it and he could take it.' The beauty of Big Arthur was that he never whined or moaned about taking a smack. He might wait years before giving one back to level up the score. Sometimes players thought that he had forgotten that he owed them one, then BANG, he would be even and they could bet their bottom dollar that before the end of the game that he was one up. But whilst mixing it with all the biff, bang and wallop he could instantly switch on and play his own exciting brand of rugby. Nothing would put him off his skilful input into a game, apart from the infamous Edouard Ponsinet incident, but more about that later.

Having been around the game for so long, I've been asked a number of times, when discussing Arthur's ability, 'Is there anyone since who could compare with Arthur?' To be honest I don't think there ever will be any one blessed with so many skills. The nearest I ever saw was a young Malcolm Reilly. He possessed a lot of the skills similar to the big man without ever having the same physical build as Arthur. Malcolm had all the tools in his bag but suffered a serious leg injury whilst playing in Australia. And although being greatly thought of down under and earning enough respect to be classed as a legend, he returned home to play on for a few seasons 'on one leg' as we used to say but he was still a brilliant player.

Arthur Clues' skills were so much in evidence that the supporters of the other teams hated him, yet in a strange way, loved him too. Stories are still told of the things he got up to both on and off the field. This big Australian moved in a circle of acquaintances that were very hard and uncompromising.

Arthur Clues first came to the attention of the rugby league world on the first post war tour of the Lions to Australia in 1946. The cream of British rugby league had made the long journey down under on the aircraft carrier Indomitable. They landed at Freemantle (because of mines around the Australian coast) and suffered an arduous journey cross country to Sydney. The last thing the players needed was to come face to face with young Arthur, a 22 year old raw boned, tough second row forward who refused to take a backward step.

It was immediately obvious that Arthur was no respecter of reputations and he had plenty of biff, bang and wallop with the huge Frank Whitcome of Bradford Northern and Wigan's rugged Ken Gee. But the most talked of battles were against the giant Doug Phillips of Oldham and Joe Egan of Wigan. His battles with the Bradford school teacher centre, big Jack Kitchen of Bradford Northern, continued more than once after he had come to play for Leeds.

Sent off in the final test in Sydney, Arthur used to tell this story of when he was called to face the disciplinary committee on the

Monday evening after the game. Arthur was shocked when the chairman of the committee said, 'Clues, we are suspending you for two matches for attacking Willie Horne on the field last Saturday. Have you anything to say?'

Arthur demanded a rethink and said, 'How can you suspend me for two matches? I was only doing what the chairman of selectors told me to do at half time, which was to clout Willie Horne as he was having a top game. Anyway I only swung one at him and that bloody missed.'

The chairman of the committee leaned forward and said, 'That's why we gave you two matches Arthur, because you bloody missed.'

Arthur was never in his life a respecter of convention. He played rugby league his way. This meant he played hard and to win at all costs. He was hated by opposing supporters and the stands and terraces would ring with their calls of, 'Dirty bugger Clues,' and 'Get that dirty sod Clues off ref.' But if those supporters' clubs ever had the chance to sign Arthur, many of those same supporters would have chipped in with money from their own pockets.

It never mattered to Arthur who the opponents were. If the opponents were in the way of Arthur's team winning then they were fair game. Those English forwards soon found out about Mr Clues, the young Sydney policeman, when he was selected for New South Wales then Australia. This was the first introduction to the English of the tough, hard nosed forward whom they would shortly meet again on the heavy, rain softened grounds of the north of England.

1

RUGBY LEAGUE, RUGBY UNION AND CRICKET

Arthur Clues was born on 2nd May 1924 in Liverpool, Australia a few miles due west of Sydney. In his early days at Parramatta Intermediate High School he played rugby league in the winter months and cricket in the summer months.

Arthur was a tall, rangy youth who left school at 14 years old and began an apprenticeship as an engineer, by which time he and his family lived in Parramatta. Also at 14 he joined the Parramatta Rugby Union Club and played in the junior sides. His rugged approach to the union game and his pace around the field soon brought him to the notice of the Parramatta committee who earmarked him for a first team place in a very short time. So impressive was his rise in skills that he made the first grade team when he was only 16 years old and when soon selected for New South Wales seconds, he was pencilled in as a future Wallaby wing forward. Arthur was tall and slender compared to the 15 stone plus big man he became later in his career. He was very mobile and standing at around 6 foot 1 inch and weighing around 12 stones he was handy enough in the rough rucking and mauling that was so much the part of Australian rugby union in those days.

To ensure that he could always be involved somewhere in the game, Arthur became a touch-judge on third team duty when the first team had the odd week off. Although the following incident is often thought of as a myth, it is actually recorded in the rugby union annals. On one occasion Arthur was running the touch for the third team when one of his mates, Lindsey Wilson, was flattened by a punch from an opponent. This alone was bad enough for the short fused touch-judge but when added to the fact that Lindsey was courting Arthur's sister (Marie), this made the incident much worse. In fact it proved too much for young Mr Clues who flung the flag away, ran onto the playing area and walloped the forward who had thumped his sister's regular date. This action started a punch up amongst almost all the players in both teams. The outcome was that Arthur was banned for life from touch-judging. He was allowed to keep playing though and from that moment he was typecast as a tough man. Unfortunately this fact meant he drew like a magnet all the idiots who played just to be a nuisance, but he saw them off and cemented his place in Parramatta's first team.

Arthur's other love, cricket, kept him active in sport all year round as he played for the Cumberland Cricket Club in Parramatta. He played in the same third grade side as the famous Richie Benaud. Arthur was a hard hitting right hand batsman who bowled a bit. He had two actions as a bowler depending on wicket conditions. These were an orthodox right hand off spin or medium paced off cutters with a bit of out-swing – which made him a dangerous opponent if the conditions were in his favour. He gained a first grade place in the side and was openly tipped to represent New South Wales as an all rounder while still a teenager. Arthur, much later in life, often said that he wished he had concentrated on his cricket skills and gone on to representative status, but he said that when he was an old man crippled in both knees.

On the rugby front at around this time, there was another urban myth concerning Arthur. This time there are two strong witnesses to testify the truth of the so-called myth. Arthur was just 18 years old and of course a central figure of the rugby team. Playing for Parramatta against, we believe, Randwick, Arthur was kicked on the head in a ruck, then kicked again at the next ruck. Realising that the same player was deliberately kicking him, he bounced up and nailed the kicker with a cracking right cross. The referee came straight in and said, 'Clues! Off for punching.'

Arthur protested: 'But that bastard kicked me twice, it's only right to give him one.' The referee insisted that Arthur walked and off he went.

Players were able to stand on the touch line after being sent off in those days. Sure enough, Arthur stood there to cheer on his team mates. But the thought of Arthur's opponent kicking him twice and the fact that Arthur only got one back began to bug him. Halfway into the second half, the kicker made a break up the touch line where Arthur stood. As the player ran past the dismissed Clues, Arthur stepped smartly about six inches onto the field and stiff arm tackled the kicker then stepped smartly back amongst his mates. The kicker was pole axed. Arthur was cited but no one came forward to accuse him. Therefore he was warned about his future conduct on the touch line and the case was dismissed. 'Ah,' the reader may say, 'one of those myths again.' Two contacts in Australia, one, a very senior citizen, who was there and another who is a trustworthy source both swear it is true.

Around January 1943, in the close season of rugby football in Australia, Arthur and a few of his mates decided to do some extra training in preparation for the coming rugby union season. They innocently asked at the Western Suburbs rugby league club if they could train with one of the teams to gain fitness. They were told they could. A couple of weeks later the players went to pay their playing fees for the coming union season to find their money was refused. They were told, 'You have trained with a professional club and by doing so have professionalized yourselves. We can not accept your playing fees as you are deemed a professional player.' So his hopes of playing for Australia at rugby union were dashed. He fancied an international cap too but decided to return to

Western Suburbs and ask for a game. At 18 years old Arthur's build was of a loose forward. He was a tough, pacy youngster with a strong defence. Wests were shrewd enough to welcome him with open arms.

He played in two second grade games to prove himself at the start of the 1943 season. These were the only times he ever played second grade rugby league, and made a two try debut against Balmain at Leichhardt Oval on 24 April 1943, just one week before his 19th birthday. His wholehearted, enthusiastic approach enabled him to play in the other 12 games for Wests' first team that season. At just 19 years old Wests must have realised that they had a star player in their hands as this tall, rangy youngster produced consistently good games week in, week out at loose forward. His explosive running from the base of the pack created many tries for his team mates and Arthur registered three tries himself in a very successful first season. He gained three representative selections too in this exciting first term. He played at loose forward for The Rest of New South Wales against the army twice and was the outstanding forward on view on both occasions. But the highest accolade was his selection for City Seconds v Country Seconds. Arthur again starred in the game and scored a superb try in the process.

Even during the war years, the system leading to international selection was similar to todays. Of course the interstate games between Queensland and New South Wales were not produced or promoted with the marketing professionalism of today's State of Origin games. In fact Queensland, although producing many great players, were decidedly second best until the introduction of origin football. Because the quality of football in Sydney was fully semi professional it was considered superior to the football played in Queensland. Therefore many good players from the North Eastern State moved south to play in Sydney. It was all about money. Almost all of the Sydney teams owned their own Leagues clubs, places where all the presentations were made after the games for every team run by the club, and there were sometimes tens of teams, all bringing in the fans. In the Leagues clubs one could buy a drink or get a meal and the slot machines were always waiting. Every weekend (and sometimes during the week), hundreds of people went to the Leagues clubs. They spent their money there meaning that every penny made the Sydney clubs richer. In Queensland slot machines were outlawed. It was against the law of the state to have them on the clubs premises. As a result a big drawing card was denied the Queensland supporters. Playing the slot machines in Sydney was an Aussie pastime.

A player moving from Queensland to Sydney was automatically eligible for selection for New South Wales, and sometimes there were more Queenslanders in the southern team than Southerners. It was obviously unfair to the Northern State and the start of the origin era introduced a vastly more competitive and fairer series. This era introduced the fire and pride seen in modern origin games. The system for higher selection was as follows. First a player was chosen for City Seconds (the first step on the ladder). Next the player might be picked for City Firsts. Both these teams played against the Seconds and Firsts country teams. City teams were selected from players who played in the city of Sydney: Eastern and Western Suburbs, Balmain, Canterbury Bankstown, South Sydney, Newtown, North Sydney and St George. The country team was chosen from teams such as Wollongong, South Newcastle, Orange, Picton, Port Kembla, Kurri-Kurri and Dorrigo. Then there would be a selection for the State sides, New South Wales or Queensland. Finally, when things returned to normal after the war, the players were selected for Australia. It was very similar to today's system of selection (the onus is now on good games in the Origin series).

So Arthur made his mark in his very first season as a

professional player and was sensational for Wests and when gaining representative honours. Although Western Suburbs had some excellent players the standard in club football was very high. In Arthur's first season, Wests could only muster three wins against 11 losses and scored 132 points in their 14 games against 175 points scored by the opposition.

About the time Arthur joined Wests he left engineering and became a policeman in the Sydney force. At first he was on traffic control and drove a motorbike and sidecar. Frank Hyde, the most respected radio and TV commentator of the time (and former North Sydney first team captain), told this story about Arthur's toughness, 'Tough?' Hyde stated, 'I'll say he was bloody tough. You always wanted him on your side but when you played against him he would knock you from pillar to post, and he is getting bigger. I saw him the other day on his police motorbike and the bugger was so big I couldn't see the bloody sidecar.'

The prestigious newspaper, *The Rugby League News* stated that, 'Two newcomers to rugby league are included in Wests side this season, lock Arthur Clues and second rower, J. Begley. Both are young men and Wests are hoping they both develop into top class players.' The paper also pointed out that because of war time conditions, the traditional jerseys of Wests, black with a white 'V', would be changed for the duration to all black. During the playing season, Arthur played rugby league for the police team on Wednesday afternoons as well as for Wests at the weekend.

The Rugby League News carried another notice of Arthur's form as the 1944 season opened. The newspaper read, 'One player who showed great promise last season and in the trials this year is Arthur Clues. He is the tireless type of player who is always on the ball and as one well known respected figure in the game said, "He is the most promising loose forward we have seen for many years."' This was praise indeed for the Wests' best find in a long time. The player also took another big step in 1944 when he played in all 14 games for Wests. This was a remarkable achievement for someone who played a very robust, uncompromising style. It speaks volumes for Arthur's fitness, high pain threshold and stamina. He also scored three tries in the 1944 campaign, which gave Wests the following playing record: played 14; won 4; drew 2; lost 8. Points for 180. Points against 244. This was a slight improvement on the previous season but there was still a long way to go.

Ray Bernasconi, one of the hard working Western Suburbs Magpies archivists, said Wests were (and still are) a very democratic club. The club was so democratic that they allowed Arthur to spend seasons 1944 and 1945 on the Wests General Committee of the club as the players' representative. He was a keen member of the Committee too. The attendance records show in 1944, Arthur missed only three meetings out of nine and came joint second in the attendance stakes just behind the top member who had eight attendances. Three representative appearances were his reward for another consistent season's work for his club. Once again he starred for the Rest of New South Wales against the army where he romped through for a good long distance try and was outstanding on defence. This game was played at the Sydney Cricket ground before 25,035 spectators and the Rest were very strongly represented against an army team that was full of Sydney first grade players. The Rest team was, Parkinson [Balmain]; Goodwin [Newtown], Bourke [Balmain], McLean [Newtown], Redmond [Newcastle]; O'Connell [Easts], Thompson [South Sydney]; Farrell [Newtown], Watt [Balmain], Montgomery [Newtown], Armstrong [South Sydney], Clues [Wests] and Hampstead [Balmain]. The Army side was, T. Kirk; P. Quinn, J. Payne, L. Smith, N. Jacobson; E. Bennett, R. Harrison; R. Dunn, J. Metcalf, C. Langton, H. Porter, W.

Mackie and L. Kelly. His promotion from City Seconds to City Firsts in only his second season in first grade rugby league showed just how much faith the top selectors had in him. Again he paid back their faith in him by turning on one of his best performances and cemented it with another fine try.

Looking at Arthur's meteoric rise to representative level, his form for Wests and his ability to turn out top big games when needed must have captivated the top selectors. The possibility of hosting a tour at home to the ever popular England side was a prospect at the end of the war, and the selectors may have been looking a couple of seasons ahead. Another honour came as Arthur was selected to play for the Metropolitan team against the army. These games against the army were played to make money for the war effort and also doubled up to give youngsters such as Arthur much needed experience. Without the tours to the UK and the reciprocal tours in Australia because of the war, the only way the young Aussie players could sharpen their teeth in representative matches was with the City v Country, various games against the Army and the rather one sided interstate games.

Arthur had crowned a fine season with his three prestigious selections. What he needed now, as the 1945 season approached, was selection for New South Wales against Queensland. As there were no test matches because of the war, the selection for New South Wales would give him the full set of honours that he could achieve at that time in representative rugby league and at only just 21 years of age. The club season for Wests in 1945 saw a vast improvement in their league position with a record of: played 15; won 8; drawn 1; lost 6. Points for 253. Points against 220. Such an improved performance earned them a play off place in the semi-finals of the premiership but they failed against Eastern Suburbs at the Sydney Cricket Ground by 28–15.

Arthur continued his excellent playing record by

appearing in 14 of the 15 games where he played and scored six tries and landed two goals. His try tally put him in second place in the clubs try scores for the season, behind J. Snare who registered 13 tries from 15 games. Then Clues' longed for selection to represent New South Wales in the interstate game finally arrived. This completed a unique sequence of continuous selections for a young and comparatively inexperienced forward. Since his City Seconds game in his first season, Arthur had played in all the available representative senior sides in two seasons. This first selection for the biggest game available to a New South Wales player, versus Queensland, coincided with the Northern State selecting Harry Bath. This must have been the first time these men locked horns as opponents. Both men later became legends in England as the best ever second row partners in representative football the country had ever seen.

The interstate game took place at the Sydney Cricket Ground before a crowd of 53,878 in horrendous playing conditions. The game was played in ankle deep, clinging mud after torrential rain. Arthur thrived in this heavy weather and produced his now-expected strong game leading New South Wales to a big 37–12 victory. Harry Bath did well enough in this first meeting and the pair clashed a couple of times as they strained to gain supremacy, one over the other. But the honours, on this day, went to Arthur. Harry Bath, dubbed universally as the best forward 'never' to play for Australia, was always the man that Arthur made a beeline for when they were in opposition. It was accepted in England that when Arthur played for Leeds or Hunslet and when Harry played for Barrow or Warrington they were the best of enemies, with no love lost. When they played together for that wonderful team that competed in the annual international matches, The Other Nationalities, they were unbeatable as a pair. To see them attacking and defending in unison it was impossible to realise the intense rivalry that existed between them. Arthur would say, 'Yeh, Bathy is a good forward but the bastard never played for Australia.' That was a man proudly defending his own title as the best back rower in the world. It was not a boast, he was stating a fact, even though the remainder of the rugby league world accepted that Harry Bath was worth a place in the Australian national side and a forward, who in England, was thought to be pretty much level with Arthur as the best in the world.

Ironically the Other Nationalities was not the first side that Arthur and Harry played in together. The following season after Arthur and Harry's first meeting, the two played together for the first time for New South Wales. Harry had joined the Balmain club from his home town club in Queensland. Arthur also figured highly in the return interstate game in Brisbane which New South Wales won again. His other representative selection was the usual pre-interstate series, the City Firsts v Country Firsts from which was selected the State side. Arthur was a first choice in the second row. He had graduated to the second row by this time in his career as he was no longer the slender 12 stone youth playing as a loose forward. His sheer size demanded a switch so he could give extra weight directly to the front row and ensure a strong scrum push. This was so important in those competitive scrimmaging days.

The end of each rugby league season brought on Arthur's other sporting love, cricket. He had established himself as a grade one batsman at his club, Cumberland in Parramatta and was still being touted as a New South Wales player in the Sheffield Shield series. The full Australian test cricket team came from this interstate competition. His team mate in third grade, Richie Benaud, was going great guns. Unfortunately Arthur's job as a policeman as well as his time-consuming rugby training and playing regime meant that something had to go. He chose to follow his rugby league instincts. But his ability to score big runs still allowed him to be amongst the first choice for the Cumberland team despite his leaning towards Wests. One of Arthur's team mates at Wests, full back Bill Keato, was also a grade one cricketer at Cumberland and the two were members of a very unique little band of grade one footballers and grade one cricketers.

The most important season of Arthur's short but successful Australian rugby league career was about to start. The 1946 season heralded the restart of the England tours of Australia and New Zealand following the end of wartime hostilities. The Australians had continued to play diluted inter state games with lots of star players away on active service. The state versus army games gave an added boost to the game down under but everyone with an interest in the game was looking forward to the start of normality again with a test series against the old sporting enemy, England. The tourists were on their way, sailing in the aircraft carrier, *Indomitable*. All the eastern seaboard of the huge continent were waiting with excitement to see the originators of this great game visit them for the first time after 10 long years. It was truly an important season – and a hectic one. The players selected for the Australian side had still to go through the selection system, City versus Country once, New South Wales against Queensland three times and New South Wales versus England twice, before selection for the big first test that was played on June 17th at the Sydney Cricket ground. There was also club football to play and to allow the big games to be fitted in, Wests only played one league game in the month of May. But despite the hectic match programme, Arthur played in all the representative games that season, as well as 11 of the 14 Wests league fixtures. His determination to do well for Wests was shown when in April he played under great difficulty with two broken ribs and, according to newspaper cuttings, was still one of the best forwards on the field. He managed five tries to be one of four joint leading try scorers for his club who, unfortunately went backwards again in their results sequence with a record of: played 14; won 4; drawn 1; lost 9. Points for 224. Points against 264.

The test team trials started with City Firsts v Country Firsts at the Sydney Cricket ground on 4th May. A curtain raiser, City Seconds v Country Seconds, was played before the Firsts game and the two Seconds Sides included some very promising players. For City, Dennis Booker [Newtown] who served Wakefield Trinity so well, was in the centre, Wally O'Connell [Eastern Suburbs] played at stand off and Keith Froome [Newtown] at scrum half – both players were Kangaroo tourists in 1948. Sid Hobson [Eastern Suburbs] and big Jack Rayner [South Sydney] formed a tough second row, Rayner being another 1948 Kangaroo and Noel Mulligan [Newtown] who would go on to a very good international career was another player who made the 1948 Kangaroo tour. The future stars for Country included, Noel Pidding, the 19 year old goal kicking full back from Maitland would later become a test star and Bob Bartlett [Wollongong] who was a classy centre who spent a few years at Bramley and Leeds. The Sydney Seconds boys proved too strong for Country Seconds and won 35–7.

The City Firsts side was almost test class with good players throughout: T. Kirk [Newtown]; L. Cooper [Eastern Suburbs], R. Bailey [Canterbury Bankstown], Joe Jorgenson [Balmain], B. Ryan [Newtown]; P. Devery [Balmain], C. Kennedy [South Sydney]; F. Farrell [Newtown], G. Watt [Eastern Suburbs], J. Spencer [Balmain], A. Clues [Western Suburbs], H. Bath [Balmain], J. Hampstead [Balmain]. Of this team, Ron Bailey, Lionel Cooper and Pat Devery went on to entertain the Huddersfield public at Fartown, Arthur Clues went to Leeds and later to Hunslet, Harry Bath came over to Barrow, then on to brilliant things at Warrington, George Watt had quite a few seasons at the Boulevard, Hull as did Bruce Ryan who moved from Hull to Leeds. The Country Firsts had good players too, Trevor Eather

[Boggabri] became a test centre, Noel White [Kurri-Kurri] also played test football on the wing, the tough Alf Gibbs [South Newcastle] made a very good test prop and Frank Johnston [Wollongong] came on the 1948 tour as a hooker along with Alf Gibbs. Again the City Firsts were too good for their 'Country Cousins' and won 31–10. Harry Bath had come down from Brisbane to sign for Balmain at the start of the 1946 campaign and played in this game as Arthur's second row partner for the first time. As these two tremendous forwards linked to pack down together, no one knew the impact they would have in representative football in England later when they were rated as the best pair ever. City Firsts had too much fire power for Country, with the two big, fast wingman Cooper and Ryan being given plenty of ball and George Watt beating Frank Johnson in the tight scrum giving the very mobile back three of Arthur Clues, Harry Bath and Jack Hampstead virtually free rein to command the middle of the field causing damage to the Country defence. Although winning comfortably, by 31–6, City had to defend strongly on occasion as Trevor Eather, Noel White and Alf Gibbs gave City one or two anxious moments.

The teams were announced for the first interstate game to be played on 11th May at the Sydney Cricket Ground. New South Wales made two changes from the successful City side, the strong running Noel White coming in for the injured Bruce Ryan on the wing and the hard working Alf Gibbs replacing Joe Spencer, who went on to reserve duty. Both replacements earned their promotion after playing well for the Country Firsts. The Queensland side was D. Dobson; P. McMahon, W. Morris, H. Melrose, L. Pegg, P. Robertson, L. Shepherd; R. Westaway, R. Rooche, R. Schultz, R. Kay, R. Stewart, C. Thornton. The Queenslanders had one or two players in their ranks that had a chance of catching the eye of the international selectors. This match was the 100th interstate match and once again brought together the Clues-

Bath partnership in the second row. The fact that they never played club rugby league with each other yet gelled when playing representative rugby tells just how good these two legends were. With Pat Devery and Clem Kennedy bossing things from the half back position and the New South Wales pack well on top, the classy home three-quarters had too much room and too much pace for the brave Queensland boys and the Southerners ran out easy, 46–10 winners.

Since his debut for New South Wales in 1945, Arthur played in all five available interstate games to the end of 1946. He was on the winning side on all five occasions. In his four seasons as a player at Wests he scored 17 tries for his club and kicked two goals. His club first grade games for Wests totalled 51 games, missing only six first team games in four seasons. Since first joining Wests, Arthur played only two games in the second grade. That was when he appeared in two trial games when first joining the club. This was an impressive and unique record for an aggressive forward. He played in 19 representative games in his four seasons and scored four tries.

The eagerly awaited England tourists arrived in Fremantle on the 6th May 1945 and played at Junee against the Southern Districts on the 22nd May. The tourists then took on Canberra in the capital city and next moved across to Sydney to tackle New South Wales on 1st June at the Sydney Cricket Ground.

Meanwhile, after the drubbing in the first interstate game the Queenslanders made a few changes for the series second game, bringing in the future Leeds favourite, Ted Verrenkamp at stand off half, P. Robinson dropping to reserve, and in the pack R. Stewart moved up to blind side prop with C. Thornton leaving loose forward to take Stewart's place in the second row. In at loose forward came the future 1948 tour vice captain, Bill Tyquin giving a stronger defensive look to the side. The Queensland team were: D. Dobson; L. Pegg, H. Melrose, W. Morris, P. McMahon; E, Verrenkamp, L. Stephens; R. Westaway, R. Roche, R. Stewart, R. Kay, C. Thornton, W. Tyquin. New South Wales too made changes for this second interstate game played on 18th May again at the Sydney Cricket Ground and offered the following team: J. Wedgwood, the Dorrigo full back who had played well for Country Firsts, Lionel Cooper, Trevor Eather the Boggabri centre, another who played well for Country, Joe Jorgenson, Noel White, Pat Devery and Keith Froome the Newtown scrum half and a future 1948 Kangaroo, 'Bumper' Farrell, Balmain hooker Herbie Gilbert, Alf Gibbs, Arthur Clues, Harry Bath and Jack Hampstead. This game saw Queensland fight back well and they had the comforting thought that they kept a tighter defence even though they lost to New South Wales yet again. This time the loss was only by 24–6, a big improvement. Reg Kay and Roy Westaway had strong games for the Northerners but the two great second rowers Clues and Bath once again held all the trump cards.

The third and final game of the series was played in Brisbane on 25th May and was the last chance for the Queensland players to stake a place in the first test team. The key men from the South also realised that they were in pole position for the international places and set about making the series a clean sweep. They did this by winning the game 30–13. One player making a big impact was the excellent full back from the Balmain club, Dave Parkinson. Beating Queensland by three games to nil was expected but this was a series from which to select the best side in Australia and only a few Queenslanders had shown the form required for that selection.

The New South Wales side had another two chances to show good form as they had to play the tourists twice before the first test on 17th June. On 1st June the England team walked out onto the fabulous Sydney Cricket ground before 51,364 spectators. Almost every spectator was yelling for their home side (wearing sky blue jerseys). This was the moment of truth for the tourists. This clash would give them an indication of how hard it would be to beat the full Aussie test team. There were a couple of surprises in the New South Wales side but all in all it looked a strong outfit with a tough front row, a superb back three, know-how in the four middle backs, a safe, experienced full back and two strong finishers on the wings. The team was: Jack Wedgwood [Dorrigo]; Lionel Cooper [Eastern Suburbs], Joe Jorgenson [Balmain], Ron Bailey [Canterbury Bankstown], Noel White [Kurri-Kurri]; Pat Devery [Balmain], Sel Lisle [Eastern Suburbs]; Frank Farrell [Newtown], George Watt [Eastern Suburbs], Jack Munn [St George], Arthur Clues [Western Suburbs], Harry Bath [Balmain], and Jack Hampstead [Balmain]. The reserves were Trevor Eather [Boggabri], Edgar Newham [Cowra], Sid Hobson [Western Suburbs] and Alf Gibbs [South Newcastle]. The tourists paid New South Wales the compliment of selecting a full strength test side to play against them with a pack that consisted of three Welsh men, a Yorkshire man and two lads from Wigan. The full England side was: Martin Ryan [Wigan]; Eric Batten [Bradford Northern], Ernest Ward [Bradford Northern], Gus Risman [Salford], Albert Johnson [Warrington]; Willie Horne [Barrow], Tommy McCue [Widnes]; Frank Whitcombe [Bradford Northern], Joe Egan [Wigan], Ken Gee [Wigan], Trevor Foster [Bradford Northern], Les White [York] and Ike Owens [Leeds]. Arthur had set his stall out to put his mark on the English 'hard men' and had early battles with the 18 stone Frank Whitcombe, the craggy Ken Gee and the tough hooker Joe Egan. Years later the wonderful, late great Trevor Foster said, 'I was fed up of being knocked over by Arthur Clues. It seemed that wherever I was, he would be there tackling me and driving me into the ground. But what a forward he was, easily the best Australian pack man.' This was the first time the poms had seen this big, rough Aussie policeman and some wished they hadn't. New South Wales took a 10–0 lead early in the second half and it looked as if a shock was looming. Tries from Eric Batten and Ike Owens plus four Gus Risman goals gave the tourists a vital win. Arthur had played his heart out and as usual had been given great support by the tough Frank Farrell, Jack Munn and Harry Bath. Harry took a high shot late in the second half and was badly concussed but the Aussies had only themselves to blame and really fancied their chances in the return.

The very next day the tourists travelled to Wollongong to play South Coast Districts and called on seven of the men who had slugged it out with New South Wales. As well as loosing that great forward, Trevor Foster, with a bad knee injury, the tourists lost by 15–12. The poor result was attributed to the hard game the tourists had played against New South Wales.

The second contest against New South Wales was on 8th June, once again at the Sydney Cricket Ground. England made only one change, bringing Doug Phillips back into the second row for the injured Trevor Foster. New South Wales made six changes, two forced on them by injuries to Harry Bath and Pat Devery. Sid Hobson [Eastern Suburbs] and Eric Bennett [Western Suburbs] stood in for Bath and Devery and Alf Gibbs [South Newcastle] came in for Jack Munn. Herbie Gilbert hooked and George Watt went to the reserves. Edgar Newham, the strong running wingman from Canterbury Bankstown came in for Noel White and Noel Mulligan [Newtown] took over from Jack Hampstead at loose forward. The full team for the second England game was Wedgwood; Cooper, Jorgenson, Bailey, Newham; Bennett, Lisle; Farrell, Gilbert, Gibbs, Clues, Hobson and Mulligan. The reserves were White, Hampstead and Watt. A good crowd of 47,085 witnessed a very professional performance by England to return to winning ways scoring a 21–7 victory. Arthur again made the English aware of his presence and had several toe-to-toe encounters with big Doug Phillips as he took on most of the English pack. Ken Gee took offence with Arthur's treatment of Joe Egan at one scrum as the big Aussie 'sent one through' out of the second row that floored the Wigan hooker. Gee challenged Arthur and Phillips joined in which brought 'Bumper' Farrell in to stand by the beleaguered Clues and the contest between the two sets of tough forwards ended as a draw. Overall the Australian selectors were satisfied with the results to date. The state side had held its own with the tourists and there was a feeling of optimism as the day of the first test drew closer.

The tourists had a scare when both selected full backs; Martin Ryan [Wigan] and Joe Jones [Barrow] went down injured and were unable to play. Skipper Gus Risman switched to full back, allowing big Jack Kitching, the Bradford schoolmaster, to come into the centre for Risman. The England team for that first crucial test was: Risman; Batten, Ernest Ward, Kitching, Johnson; Horne, McCue; Whitcombe, Egan, Gee, White, Phillips and Owens. The test match turned out to be a most controversial affair. Firstly the Aussies went for a team that looked good enough to win it at a canter. Harry Bath was ruled out with the head injury but still the pack was big, strong and skilful. Dave Parkinson had done enough in the third interstate game to warrant a place. Edgar Newham held off some top credentials from Noel White and Bruce Ryan to get a wing spot. John Grice from South Brisbane claimed the number seven jersey. The full side was: D. Parkinson [Balmain]; Lionel Cooper [Eastern Suburbs], Joe Jorgenson [Balmain], Ron Bailey [Canterbury Bankstown], Edgar Newham [Cowra]; Pat Devery [Balmain], John Grice [Souths, Brisbane]; Frank Farrell [Newtown], George Watt [Eastern suburbs], Roy Westaway [Valleys, Brisbane], Arthur Clues [Western Suburbs], Reg

Kay [Souths, Brisbane] and Noel Mulligan [Newtown]. Reserves were Eric Bennett [Western Suburbs] and Jim Armstrong [South Sydney].

The test started in true tradition as Arthur clashed with Joe Egan in centre field. The crowd of 64,527 sensed a game to remember was taking place before them. A scrum some 30 yards out from Australia's line was won by England and Tommy McCue fed Willie Horne just the ball he liked. The pass put Horne on the outside of Devery (the Aussie stand off) and Horne was round his opposite number in a flash, a devastating side step on Parkinson and the Barrow maestro was over. During this test Gus Risman had a nightmare of a kicking game and missed eight out of nine shots at goal. Arthur was a constant thorn in England's side and another dust up, this time with the giant Doug Phillips, had the huge crowd roaring. Joe Jorgenson kicked a neat penalty goal as the Aussies turned the screw and Arthur was held up on the English try line after a strong break. But the rotund Whitcombe used his bulk to carry three tacklers over the line to put England 6–2 in front. Then, on 30 minutes, Jack Kitching went down in a tackle with Joe Jorgenson and the Bradford centre appeared to punch his Aussie opponent on the ground. A scuffle occurred and when it was settled, Mr McMahon the referee dismissed Kitching. Big Jack claimed he had been bitten but Mr McMahon would have nothing to do with that and insisted that Kitching must go. Kitching attempted to show anyone around the marks on his chest and arm but he was off and England had a huge task to face – 50 minutes of aggression with a man short. Sensing that the English forwards were tiring Clues, Kay and Mulligan surged toward the tourists' line with short passing and close support. They were held but from this attack Ron Bailey straightened onto a Devery pass and, showing neat side steps off both feet, rounded Ike Owens and Willie Horne to dance over the try line to score. It was 6–5 to England and Risman kicked his only goal of the afternoon from a penalty, making the score 8–5. The game was swaying end to end and the almost 65,000 crowd went berserk when Lionel Cooper fielded a kick through some 60 yards from the English line and set off on one of those runs that the supporters of the Huddersfield club remember so vividly even now after all those years. Running along the touch line he smashed past McCue and stepped inside of the despairing Owens' tackle. Veering infield, Cooper approached the England captain, Risman. Going in towards the full back, Cooper suddenly side stepped away and left Risman grasping thin air as the big wingman raced over for a memorable try. From absolute pandemonium the crowd fell into a hushed silence as, with the score at 8 points all, Jorgenson teed up the ball for the kick to put Australia in front for the first time in the game. The Aussie centre swung his leg and struck the ball sweetly but it veered away in the last seconds of flight and went wide of the posts. Further fights started as Frank Farrell and Arthur set about the Englishmen who were out on their feet. Gee smacked Arthur and Australia were awarded a penalty straight in front of the posts, about 20 yards out. With only a few minutes left, Jorgenson placed the ball intending to give Australia the first crucial test win but before a stunned partisan crowd he inexplicably sliced the ball wide and the siren went to declare a drawn match, 8 points all. The controversy continued as Jack Kitching told the biting story to the Aussie press and they headlined it in Monday morning's newspapers. Jorgenson was incensed and threatened to take legal action against Kitching. To save the tour, Mr Popplewell, the Leeds market gardener and tour football manager, used his power of personality and smoothed over a delicate problem. One or two of the English forwards mentioned the aggressive attitude of Arthur Clues and almost every tourist had something to say to the newspapers about the big, tough Wests enforcer. All the tourists admitted they wished he played for them in England. Jim Lewthwaite, one of only three surviving 'Indomitables' (the others were Joe Egan and Bryn Knowelden) said of Arthur in those days, 'He wasn't a man to tangle with but you wanted him on your side if the truth were known.'

The Australian team knew they had missed a great chance of going one up in the series but it was still 'even-steven' with all to play for. The second test, played in Brisbane on 6th July at the old Exhibition Ground was marketed well and a big crowd was expected, especially as the first test was such a close run thing. As one might expect, Australia maintained the same side that should have won the game in Sydney except at loose forward where Jack Hutchinson [Newcastle] replaced the injured Mulligan. The English played the same pack, which did a superb job in the first test but made several changes to the backs. Ernest Ward moved to full back, allowing Risman to operate in his favourite position of centre. The other centre berth was taken by the big Welshman who played for Wigan, Ted Ward. Arthur Bassett, the big Halifax policeman came onto the wing for Eric Batten who had a slight injury. Bassett was on test debut. Local Brisbane newspapers told of a sell out which made the attendance the biggest crowd for any sport within the city of Brisbane. With such a big crowd to handle the stewarding was inadequate and at least another 12,000 gained unofficial entrance.

The game, although close enough, was swept away from Australia by the power and pace of the two English wingmen. Bassett scored three tries out of the top drawer, one a spectacular effort in which he beat five would be tacklers and never deviated from running close to the touch line. His other two tries were worth paying to see too as he displayed skill, pace and power to reach his objective. Albert Johnson chipped in with another long range, side stepping try as the tourists gave the Aussies a lesson in how to win a test match. Australia could not cope with the English teamwork and although Arthur, Reg Kay and Roy Westaway were strong forwards and there was always the threat of Lionel Cooper and Pat Devery, it was England's day. Cooper did his usual by blitzing over for a great try and Jorgenson landed one goal but it was not enough to counter the 14 points built up by the tourists. Late in the game, Arthur and his antagonist, Joe Egan, swapped a few punches after a play the ball and Joe was sent off. It was an ongoing saga with these two players, plus Phillips and Gee. The match ended with a 14–5 win for England.

Throughout the duration of the test series, the topic of conversation in the Australian dressing room concerned the fact that in 1947 Parramatta would enter the senior Sydney league as a bona fide club. This meant that by the rules of the Sydney competition, any player who lived in Parramatta had to play for that club. Arthur would have to leave Wests and play for the area in which he resided. He didn't want to play for Parramatta but would be forced to do so if he stayed where he was. He was still a policeman in Sydney, though that would not change, and was earning $17 per week. His pay at Wests was around $6 per win (possibly half that if beaten). Arthur was unsettled to say the least, but it didn't show in his play. The tourists frequently discussed what a player he would be back in England. The Leeds club had two players on tour, Ike Owens and Dai Jenkins, two Welshmen who were key players at Leeds. Owens was to gain the reputation of being possibly the best loose forward who had yet toured Australia on this 1946 trip. Rumour has it that Ike Owens tipped off the Leeds representative in Australia, John 'Dinny' Campbell about Clues. Campbell was a former Leeds centre, who acted for the club, signing many excellent Australian players. Owens wondered if the Leeds club were interested in the big, tough man. Campbell, a shrewd judge of a footballer was interested indeed and contacted the board at Headingley with a recommendation that Clues should be signed as soon as possible. This was mainly down to his glowing performance against England and the fact that he was unsettled about the Parramatta issue. Several Australian players were potentially making the pilgrimage to the United Kingdom. Ron Bailey had tipped off Huddersfield about the big, strong Lionel Cooper and the superb footballer Pat Devery.

The Aussies had to win the third test at the Sydney Cricket Ground on 20th July to salvage something from the series. England made changes both in the backs and in the pack. Eric Batten returned to the exclusion of Albert Johnson and George Curran replaced Frank Whitcombe at prop. The side was: Ernest Ward; Batten, Risman, Ted Ward, Bassett; Horne, McCue; Gee, Egan, Curran, White, Phillips and Owens. Australia brought in Trevor Eather [Boggabri] for Ron Bailey in the centre, Noel White [Kurri-Kurri] in for Edgar Newham on the wing, Clem Kennedy [South Sydney] at scrum half for John Grice, Jack Hutchinson made way for Noel Mulligan who was fit again at loose forward and Roy Westaway was left out to make way for Jim Armstrong [South Sydney] at prop. Armstrong was a heavyweight wrestler who represented Australia in the 1948 London Olympics and won the bronze medal. He won the gold medal in the 1950 Empire Games and a silver medal in the Commonwealth Games of 1962. The Australian side was: Parkinson; Cooper, Jorgenson, Eather, White; Devery, Kennedy; Farrell, Watt, Armstrong, Clues, Kay and Mulligan. But despite the Aussie reshuffle, England went on to gain their biggest win of the test series with a 20–7 victory. The brave Aussies were leading at half time by 7–2 after a blistering try by Clem Kennedy and two goals kicked by Joe Jorgenson to a Risman penalty goal. The second half was all England with Arthur Bassett crashing over for two excellent tries and George Curran and Ike Owens adding two more. Another two goals from Gus Risman and one goal from Ted Ward meant a 20–7 win for the tourists. Arthur Clues was sent off for 'missing' Willie Horne on 60 minutes. The bravest incident of the match was Dave Parkinson's noble effort to play on after Arthur was dismissed so as not to leave his team mates with 11 men. Parkinson went to hospital after the game and found that he had broken a bone in his leg. He must have been in agony. Gus Risman was far from kind in his post-test interview stating that when the Australians had found they could not match England at pure rugby, they resorted to roughhouse tactics.

So the adventure was over. Australia had lost the series at home. Arthur had made a huge name for himself. The interstate games plus the test matches had thrust him into the limelight. He was still only just 22 years old and had mixed it with the best, both when playing football and for standing his ground. The 1946 season had ended in Australia but the season was about to begin in England. The tourists were travelling back to face nine months of hard rugby, most of it spent ankle deep in mud and in freezing conditions. This was so different from the recent months in the Southern Hemisphere playing on firm true grounds. Arthur played his last game for Wests against Canterbury Bankstown on 17th August 1946 at Pratten Park. No one knew then that it was to be his last ever game in Australia.

Although Arthur returned to cricket after a season of representative and club rugby league, he had a lot on his mind. Several clubs had contacted him to discuss him going to England to play football. One approach was from Leeds RLFC whose ground was not only the home of Yorkshire Cricket Club but also regularly housed test matches. The ground was well known to the king of Australian test batsmen, Don Bradman. Arthur had much to do if he was to go to the United Kingdom. He had to give notice in his job as a policeman, tidy up things with his family and friends. He also had to notify Wests of his departure. He discussed the Leeds' terms with Dinny Campbell. Their top offer was a five year contract with a signing fee of £750. Match terms were £7 for a win, £6 for a draw and £5 for a loss. In the end, Clues' forced signing for the new club, Parramatta, was the major reason he left Australia. He had also seen the speed a player could be scrapped after his best days had gone. He openly said in one interview, 'I knew that when my turn came they would not want to know me. I had seen too many old timers who had given their all for Australian rugby league just put out to grass and all the back slapping in the world won't pay the rent. I loved playing for Australia but I must think of tomorrow.'

He made his decision to go to Leeds. Wests were terribly disappointed and one article in the local newspaper read, 'Wests suffered a blow when Arthur Clues, the rising young forward who has already represented Australia in three Tests against England, left the club to join the Leeds club in England.'

Meanwhile back in Leeds the newspapers could only offer gossip as forms had not yet been signed. The word was that Leeds were hot on the trail of two players from the Southern Hemisphere, one a goal kicking rugby union full back from New Zealand and the other a big, young second rower from Australia. Rumours were heard in pubs, greengrocers' shops and in barbers' chairs. No one could be sure if the rumours were true. Then in December 1946 the headlines hit the *Yorkshire Evening Post*, 'Leeds sign New Zealander Bert Cook.' Bert Cook from Hawkes Bay had played at Headingley for the New Zealand Services team in a rugby union game and had caught the eye of the Leeds directors with his faultless fielding, prodigious punts and immaculate goal kicking. The Post carried another headline the evening after, 'Another signing Imminent.'

In early January 1947 came the official news that the Leeds club had signed, Arthur Charles Clues. Page 181 of the minute book of the Leeds RLFC board of directors details the plan to bring Arthur over. Dated 7th January 1947, motion number two reads: 'Cablegram from Campbell. Clues leaves Sydney on January 18th on flight Lancastrian ... Pay BOAC London £300 Stirling. Request them to advise Qantas Sydney. Await conformation.' So he would soon be on his way. I remember my late father telling me about his arrival from a statement in the *Yorkshire Evening Post*. 'He's coming,' he announced, 'it won't be long now. I bet Joe Egan and Ken Gee are rubbing their hands,' my Dad said, no doubt thinking that the two Wiganers would be wanting some payback time against Arthur for what he gave them in the recent tests. All the talk was about Arthur arriving: kids discussed it at our school; people speculated about it at the Sacred Heart on Burley Road. The Sacred Heart was only a good drop kick away from the holy of holies, Headingley. People there couldn't wait for the news that Arthur was ready to train. Four kids from my neighbourhood never missed a training night. We would stand outside the old dressing room door, just at the top of the ramp that led directly onto God's green acre, the pitch. Our favourite players at the time were Walt Best (a local wingman who was signed from Bradford Northern), Dickie Williams (the excellent Welsh stand off half), Tommy Cornelius (another Welshman who was a utility back), Gareth Price (a classy centre with a splayed leg action when running and the third Welshman of many on the Leeds books at that time) and Alf Watson (a Castleford lad who had been a prisoner of war in Europe who was a cracking loose forward or second rower). Arthur was joining a team that would not have been out of place in Cardiff as the other men from the principality included Dai Jenkins and Ike Owens (both members of the 1946 tour), Dai Prosser, T.L. (Les) Williams, Con Murphy and Cliff Carter. There were nine Welshmen and all were good players.

It was January and although we expected the weather to be cold we were almost halfway through the winter and had seen little snow. There was a strange feeling in the air as though someone had left the outside door open. It was not freezing but there was always a steady cold feeling down our backs. The newspaper headlines told us what we had been waiting for: 'Clues arrives today.' Bert Cook made his debut against York on 18th January 1947 at Headingley and in a 26–7 win had kicked four goals. Tuesday 28th January saw what seemed like hundreds of youngsters milling around the dressing room door as the Leeds players inside changed into their training gear. That evening's newspaper said that if Arthur proved fit enough, he would make his debut in the second row against Hull at home next Saturday (1st February). Frank 'Dolly' Dawson was the Leeds coach and the tough, well respected former Hunslet forward was well known for his hard, fit forwards. Arthur would have to be fit to get into Dolly's team.

I was aching to see Arthur. 'He must be at least 8 feet tall and weigh around 25 stone as he's knocked out all the England forwards with one punch,' that's the sort of stuff we said as the clock on the pavilion roof showed 6.45pm through the murk of that bitterly cold February evening. That was the starting time for training and Dolly was always punctual. It was noisy as the kids were bored waiting when suddenly a strange hush fell across those rowdy kids as the dressing room door opened, just an inch or two. The bloke inside had obviously been told to wait a second, then the door swung wide open as out walked Dickie Williams talking to the next man out in a serious manner. The rest of the Leeds team came out next, all muffled up against the unyielding cold blast of freezing air that had arrived with a vengeance that morning and never let up all day. The man who came out with Dickie Williams stood talking to the stand off half at the top of the ramp which led onto the field. He was big, not 8 feet tall, but big. As he came out of the dressing room the kids who had been milling around had stopped and parted, just like the Red Sea did for Moses. Now the banks of the sea were all ears trying to hear this big man talk. As he turned to go down the ramp I stood about six feet from him. I can remember to this day what he was wearing. He wore a thick, heavy polo neck sweater in a grey colour (goalkeeper's jumpers we used to call them), and a pair of maroon track suit bottoms with the legs tucked into the tops of a pair of Leeds football socks. He turned to go down the ramp and as he did he looked straight at me and winked. All the other kids said he winked at them but I knew he had winked at me!

The players did several laps of the rugby field and then went under the South Stand, onto the cinder running track that ran the full length of the stand, about 85 yards long. We were allowed to stand near enough to look in awe at the pace these big men ran at. At this stage, Arthur seemed to be just ordinary. Then Dolly called for the last four sprints to be full out and we saw the big man run and my, could he run. In the final four sprints Arthur ran against two forwards and two backs and beat them all, although the two backs were with him at the line he just made the tape first. Then the players went out to the cricket field and ran an uncountable number of laps, round and round. Dolly stopped them after an age and gathered the group of players around him to discuss the coming Saturday's game. Then he gave the players a change. He sent them lapping again but in the opposite direction to the first laps.

I started seriously supporting Leeds at the start of the 1946 season. I went to Headingley with my Dad when he was home on leave from the army to watch war time rugby and can remember him taking me to see an inter services rugby union game in January 1943. Later I realised that most players in one particular team were rugby league players. In all honesty I can just remember two teams running around on the pitch. But we did see a bit of rugby league. Also my Dad's mate took us to Dewsbury once in a motorbike and sidecar to see rugby but again I couldn't say who played. It was just men running around. The Leeds team just before Arthur arrived included men such as Cliff Evans, Idwal Davies, Billy Banks, Bob Batten, Jack Kelly, Bernard Gray, Jack Booth, Des Foreman, Jack Newbound and just as he was about to retire, Ken Jubb. The backbone of the side was in place after the arrival of Bert Cook who fitted in wonderfully well. Gareth Price showed consistent form and Dickie Williams and Dai Jenkins combined superbly with the fast, strong and skilful Ike Owns, thereby supplying that crucial triangle at the base of the pack. Two men who had spent most of the hostilities as prisoners of war, Alf Watson and Reg Wheatley, recovered to become key forwards just as Arthur arrived.

Arthur made his debut for Leeds on 1st February 1947 against the very strong Hull FC at Headingley on a sodden pitch in an Arctic cold wind. The Leeds team that fateful day was Bert Cook; Walt Best, Gareth Price, Tommy Cornelius, Ernie Whitehead; Dickie Williams, Dai Jenkins; Chris Brereton, Con Murphy, Dai Prosser, Alf Watson, Arthur Clues and Ike Owens. Hull won the mud bound encounter by 9–2, Bert Cook kicking the penalty goal for the only points for Leeds of the afternoon. The weather caught Arthur by surprise and he had difficulty coming to terms, not so much with the mud, as he had played in games at home after tropical winter storms, but with the fact that it was cold mud. It was the cold which unsettled him most of all. He showed potential and worked hard at keeping in the game as the cold penetrated his body and more importantly his hands. All in all it was an acceptable debut without telling what memorable performances he would produce later.

The game ended and no more matches were played until some five weeks later because the cold that we had all felt for several weeks had been followed by the coldest, snowiest period in living memory, the Arctic winter of 1947. It arrived first as a medium fall of snow on Monday 3rd February. Usually the air became a little warmer but the icy wind I had felt weeks before the snow was still there. Then on Wednesday we awoke to another heavy snow fall, this time the snow fell all day. I remember those whose Mums were not working or who could go to grandparents or neighbours were allowed out of school early. Leaving school in the already darkening February mid-afternoon we found to our delight that it was still snowing. I mention that bad winter to make the point that Arthur must have wondered what he had come to. There were pictures in the evening newspapers of Arthur eating the snow as the media tried everything to maintain the interest that Bert Cook's and Arthur Clues' signings had generated. Then it stopped snowing, but it was followed by the frost! The roads in and around the city of Leeds were chaotic.

March came along. Then it snowed heavily again. To illustrate just how much snow certain areas around Leeds had, I recall one incident vividly. My Dad worked for the delivery department of the LMS railway and started work at 7.00am every morning, Monday to Saturday. It would have been a Monday morning when my Dad gently woke me to say that it had snowed again and that he wanted me to see just how deep it was. All the windows were frozen over inside the glass and it was so cold that my Dad had a blanket with him in which he wrapped me and carried me downstairs. He stood me up to watch him open our house door. We lived in a scullery house in one of the hundreds of streets below the Headingley ground. Our door opened straight out into the street and when my Dad gently opened the door, the snow had drifted half way up it. I stood looking at a 4 foot high wall of snow and in that snow was the perfect indent of our door's moulded panels. It was like a half white door of clean snow. In the streets and roads the snow lay about 15 inches deep but my Dad was left with the daunting task of digging himself out to go to work. All he had in the house was a small coal shovel. He did get out (the workmen in those days were very conscientious) and I remember him saying that of all the men who worked for his department only one was late for work that day.

The problem with this particular winter was not so much

the snow but the deep frost every day and particularly at night. The snow falls became lighter, but because of the deep frost, the snow already on the ground built up and froze every day. We 'cleared our flags' outside our house every evening and threw the snow into the side of the street but soon we could not see across to our neighbours' houses, only a matter of 10 yards away because of the height of the moved snow. And so it went on. Every day meant the same cold walk to school and a colder walk back in the afternoon. The biggest problem of all was that there was no rugby. The date for the first round cup ties came and went with no respite in the cold Arctic weather. Leeds had drawn the tough, no nonsense Barrow side in the first round and in those days the first round was on a two leg basis. One game was played at home and the following weekend the return game was played on the opponents' ground. There was little hope of any sort of game within the foreseeable future with so much snow around. And if the snow ever began to thaw, a bigger problem would be drainage.

A month passed from Arthur's debut and still the snow remained. The days became a little warmer and a slow daytime thaw set in, Of course the night frost cancelled out any thaw. Finally there was light at the end of the tunnel as warmer weather was forecasted in two weeks. Attitudes suddenly changed and folk began to shake off the winter blues even though the snow still lay thick on the ground. The league programme had fallen five weeks behind with the layoff and each week the message from Headingley was they would move to get the ground ready as soon as possible. The official date for the Leeds v Barrow first leg was 8th February. This date had long since gone. The word was that the game might go ahead on 8th March if the promised thaw came. The club set about clearing the ground with enthusiasm. They cleared snowdrifts from the pitch and the terraces and laid straw over the pitch to stop the frost. This operation cost the club £400 (a tidy sum in those days) and the officials crossed their fingers that no further heavy falls of snow would occur.

2

UP AND RUNNING AGAIN, ALL THE WAY TO WEMBLEY

At long last the waiting was over. Although the snow still covered the streets, roads and parks around the Headingley district, the workers had performed miracles on the field and terraces up at the ground. Whilst 8th March 1947 dawned grey and foreboding, it seemed a milestone for the youngsters that rugby league was up and running. It seemed that the cold, dark days, when the snow fell so heavily that it obliterated everything in a grey and white background, were on their way out. Or so we thought! Arthur wrote an article in the *Evening Post* saying how much he was looking forward to playing again. Of course all the kids at school read it and added bits to it, as kids do. My school mate and I arrived early at Headingley as usual and we stood outside the main gates in the narrow St Michaels Lane, hoping to see our heroes walking into the ground (the players used to walk as there were few cars in those days). Then we went into the ground behind the South Stand to the schoolboy's enclosure clutching a match programme. There had been a heavy frost again overnight but the one inch covering of snow still on the ground, left there by the workforce so that the turf was not dug into, plus the generous covering of new straw, had kept old Jack Frost at bay. The ground was very soft indeed when the army of men had cleared the straw to the sides of the pitch. This straw, by the way, was used as a rugby pitch at half time by the hundreds of kids who tackled their hearts out, mimicking big Arthur and Dai Prosser, as they dived about taking a soft landing in the straw.

The £400 was well spent by the Leeds board of directors on preparing the ground as the official attendance at this mouth watering cup tie was just a tad over 26,000. Arthur did not feel lonely in this game. Once again he had as his loose forward, the brilliant Ike Owens who had departed from the 1946 tour with the reputation of being the best loose forward ever seen in Australia and a man whom Arthur tangled with several times in the three tests. Now Ike was his mate. Another 1946 tourist that Arthur had met on many occasions was the crafty Leeds scrum half, the great footballer, Dai Jenkins. Playing for Barrow were four of the recent tourists, Joe Jones at full back (safe as the Bank of England the Barrow public used to say), the great international wingman, Jim Lewthwaite (who had said earlier that all the tourists had wished Arthur had been on their side), Bryn Knowelden (the experienced and excellent stand off or centre who went on to play for Warrington) and the magnificent legend at stand off, Willie Horne (whom Arthur had attempted to decapitate in the final test). Barrow were a tough side which included two of the most outstanding wingmen of their age, Jim Lewthwaite and Roy Francis. The pack was big, strong and young and they were renowned cup fighters. In Horne and Bowyer the 'Shipbuilders' had a great pair of half backs too so Leeds' task was a tough one, especially as this first round was a two legged affair.

As expected the pitch turned quickly into a quagmire. One would think this was totally alien to Horne's silky skills but this superb footballer had a copybook game and proved that great footballers can play on anything. The teams in this electrically charged match were, Leeds: Cook; Cornelius, Price, T.L. Williams, Whitehead; Dickie Williams, Jenkins; Brereton,

Murphy, Prosser, Clues, Watson and Owens. The Barrow team were: Jones; Lewthwaite, Knowelden, Bowker, Francis; Horne, Bowyer; Longman, Woods, Hornby, Ayres, Jenkins and Stone. The referee was the much respected Mr Charlie Appleton [Warrington].

As both teams had been out of action for five weeks it was to be expected that there was a 'testing out' period. Prosser, Watson, Brereton and Arthur revelled in these heavy conditions. The strong Longman, Hornby, Stone and Ayres gave as much as they received and it soon developed into a ding-dong struggle. Cook chimed into the Leeds three-quarter line from a scrum and his bulk almost brought the first score but Stone and Bowker nailed him inches short. Price went near but the Barrow pack would not surrender and Ayres, Jenkins and Stone pushed Leeds back for Horne to pick his time expertly to drift into the game and bring the very swift Francis into action with a magnificent touch line run, stopped with great effort by Cook and Cornelius. During this game the famous Arthur Clues' side step was seen. The late Ken Dalby the Leeds historian and former coach at the club describes in his book *The Headingley Story, volume 4*, 'A mighty side stepping lunge by Clues.' It was mighty indeed and this was just the type of ground Arthur loved to use the move on. Three or four times he stepped like a ballroom dancer over the top of the morass of mud, as if gliding into a gap. The much lighter Leeds backs found the clinging mud too much of an obstacle and the big man was stopped by the speedy Horne and Jones each time with no support. Leeds slogged it out through the mud to a position where Clues and Watson found enough time to inter-pass and Watson found the unmarked Cornelius who coolly dropped a fine goal out of the ankle deep sludge with his trusty left boot. The teams turned around and headed for the dressing rooms at half time to change into clean, dry kit, with the game still wide open at

2–0 in Leeds' favour.

The players emerged after the interval with clean jerseys, shorts and faces after washing in hot water. Within seconds they were mud covered again, the distinctive blue and white hoops of Barrow and the tangerine jerseys of Leeds appeared all the same colour after the first tackle of the second half becoming just as muddy as before. Bert Cook was in masterly form with his touch finding and his huge punt put a scrum down only 10 yards from the Barrow line. Con Murphy won the ball and from this position Leeds launched a series of attacks which saw Arthur being hurled back from the line twice in as many minutes. Dai Prosser, a very strong man, went close, as did Alf Watson. Having worked the ball into the right hand corner, Leeds swung the ball to their left and the local lad Ernie Whitehead went for the corner flag bravely. Joe Jones halted him inches short. Barrow were almost out on their feet as Leeds fired the passing back to their right and the overlap came as Gareth Price drew in Roy Francis and slipped a superb pass to Tommy Cornelius who went in about half way between posts and corner flag. Cook landed a great conversion considering the muddy conditions.

Another aspect of the great man's skills was on show for the first time as Arthur kicked tactically for Whitehead to chase into the corner. The tremendous pace of Francis saved Barrow as both wingmen dived for the ball in the in-goal area and Francis finger tipped the ball into dead to save the day. Another great 30 yards break by Arthur after another brilliant side step set up a chance for the speedy Ike Owens who raced diagonally towards the Barrow line after taking Arthur's pass. As he prepared to take a shallow dive to score, Stone and Knowelden tackled him simultaneously. As Stone was underneath Owens, it stopped him grounding the ball and all three men slid through the mud and over the dead ball line. The question was whether seven points would be enough to take up to Barrow in the second leg. Barrow were a tough team to beat on their own Craven Park ground and with their hard cup tie reputation there were people in the crowd who thought that Leeds needed more than the seven points advantage they were holding right now. The tension was broken as Leeds stormed the Barrow line again after a period of strong defensive work as Horne had Lewthwaite challenging at the flag, only for Cook and Whitehead managing to push the big wingman into touch. Once again, Horne had Francis sprinting clear but a terrific cover tackling effort by both Clues and Watson caught the speeding Barrow wingman as he looked to be pulling clear. But the tension eased as Dai Jenkins made unbelievable ground in the morass. Alf Watson carried the ball on to the supporting Arthur Clues who sent Owens away to draw Jones and send Price striding over with two men spare on his outside. Leeds had a precious 12 point lead to take to Barrow but it was hardly a forgone conclusion that it would be enough.

The weather had become overcast again with those dreadful light grey clouds at nightfall, the kind of clouds that threaten snow. The frost was still prevalent at night and the forecast suddenly became worrying as the weatherman said there was a chance of further heavy falls of snow. The daunting thing about it was that Leeds had to travel to the North West coast to play the second leg on Thursday 13th March, not knowing for certain if the game was on or off. Barrow had seen another medium fall of snow on Tuesday and considered that if no more snow fell there was a great chance of the game being on. Leeds decided to travel up on Wednesday afternoon and stay overnight at Grange-over-Sands. This gave them a good starting base ahead of the game at Barrow. Secretary 'George' Hirst travelled late with two players, Dai Jenkins and Con Murphy, arriving late evening on Wednesday to find the hotel almost blocked in by a severe snow storm and high winds causing drifts. Craven Park, Barrow, was finally ruled out late Wednesday evening after another heavy snow fall and the alternative venue, Wigan's Central Park, was also very doubtful. The snow had created mayhem again. Heavy snow was reported from Headingley. The problem had to be faced and decisions made quickly. The headache was partly resolved by an agreement that if an early morning phone call to Wigan found the pitch unfit and the pitch at Headingley could be cleared, then the Barrow team would be on the 9.00am train to Leeds and the game would be played again at Headingley on Thursday evening. But if the ground at Headingley was not fit, then Leeds would go through to the second round on the strength of their 12–0 victory in the first leg.

The early morning call found Central Park covered in six inches of snow so the Leeds team set off, through the drifts, to Leeds. The conditions were so bad that after many hairy, sliding, near misses, and travelling non-stop, they arrived at Headingley at 4.00pm. The directors expected a heavy fine at least, or even disqualification from the competition for being so late despite being 'at home'. But the news that Barrow had not travelled was greeted with mixed feelings on arrival at the Pavilion. It had been decided that the tie would be played on Saturday 15th March at Headingley.

The weather did not inhibit the faithful rugby league supporters. Over 26,000 streamed into ground and were amazed that the snow had been cleared once again in a professional manner and that the straw had done its job. The Leeds team played the same team as in the first leg, satisfied that the job could be finished with the side that did so well last time in the mud. Barrow though had an enforced change at scrum half when Bowyer was declared unfit and Little, a scrum half of great experience and a tremendous pre war player for Barrow, deputised for him. In the pack, Scott, a former Leeds forward, and Grainger came in for Hornby at prop and Stone at loose forward. Leeds continued to wear their tangerine coloured jerseys with blue shorts. The traditional colours of blue jersey with an irregular amber hoop across chest and arms must have been unavailable because of the shortage of materials after the war. The tangerine with blue must have been the nearest colours available to blue and amber. I wonder what Arthur and Bert Cook made of the English weather? Bert played in only three games in eight weeks and Arthur played only two games in five weeks.

The Barrow side for the second leg was: Jones; Lewthwaite, Knowelden, Bowker, Francis; Horne, Little; Longman, Woods, Scott, Ayres, Jenkins, and Grainger. The referee was Mr W. Hemmings [Halifax]. Barrow led the way in the early exchanges as the Leeds pack, once again, came to terms with the ankle deep mud and adjusted to playing with a ball as slippery as a bar of soap at bath time. Prosser, once more, was a mighty man and gloried in the conditions. Arthur too had the Barrow tacklers backing off him as they expected that superb side step every time he handled the ball. And because they backed off him he produced some telling breaks in midfield. Another aspect of his play was his support of the ball carrier. If a fellow forward made any sort of inroad into the opponents' line, usually the first man up in support was Arthur, who then had the awareness to hand on to a back and also the pace, if necessary, to run the ball himself. The 12 point lead from the first leg looked good even early in the game as the morass that normally looked so lush and green pulled everyone, except Francis and Lewthwaite, down to the same pace as the game developed into a massive slog. Horne was as usual a dangerous player. He continuously attempted to release both his match winning wingmen with shrewd kicking in behind the Leeds forwards. The occasional long pass, delivered in this sea of mud with unbelievable expertise, was a constant danger. Leeds were awarded a penalty as the Barrow second row man, Ayres clashed with Arthur after the big Aussie had been knocked down with a late tackle. Even the master kicker Cook was finding it difficult to control his non kicking foot as he connected with the dead ball. But the Kiwi decided to have a shot at goal from some 35 yards out and at an angle. Cook struck the ball well but in the last few yards it veered in flight, struck the upright post and bounced back into the field of play. Joe Jones was covering the post, as good full backs did, and caught the rebound. He set off down field but Bert Cook had chased his own kick and challenged Jones just inside his own 25 area. As Jones was attempting to hold off Cook, he dropped the ball and the ever alert Dai Jenkins scooped it up and scurried the 15 yards to the line for an opportunist's try. Cook missed with the conversion but in conditions like this, the three points for the try were priceless.

The Barrow team was now 15 points down, counting the 12 points from the first leg. Their body language was negative. Their performance deteriorated a few minutes before half time as Dai Jenkins took on his opposite number, Little, and left him sprawling with a dummy and a burst of pace, Alf Watson came up on the half back's shoulder when Jones offered his tackle on Jenkins and went clear. The remnants of the cover were closing in on Watson and his smartly timed pass sent Arthur Clues away, seemingly a certain scorer. But the super fast Francis pulled back on Clues who was strong enough to stand the impact of the wingman's challenge and passed to Price who strolled over wide out.

Normally the teams in those days stayed out on the field at half time but the conditions were so bad that a change of kit and a wash in hot water was required. The players went into the dressing rooms. With an 18 point lead, Leeds looked home and dry (pardon the pun).

In the second half, Barrow tried all they knew to pull something out of the game. The disruption to training because of the snow, the psychological strain of the on-off second leg and the very unusual situation of loosing the home tie of the two legged first round all took a toll on the side physically and mentally. And try as they might they could not break the hold on the game that this confident Leeds side had. The Leeds forwards became the dominant force in the second half with Arthur, Dai Prosser, Alf Watson and Ike Owens playing outstanding rugby. In the context of open running football, unfortunately the weather won the day. As in the first leg, the crucial victory was in the fight to get the match on. The gratitude of the Leeds team's supporters no doubt went to their good pack of forwards who took on the excellent Barrow six and won the two games, albeit both at Headingley, on a glue-pot of a pitch.

The second round of the Challenge Cup was a new experience in more ways than one for Arthur. He was going deeper into arguably the best knock out cup in the world and, according to the old stagers in the Leeds side, each game from now would get more difficult. Because of the loss of five weeks' football, the second and third rounds of the cup took precedence over the league matches. Therefore cup tie followed cup tie on three consecutive weekends. The second round draw had thrown together yet another first for him in this country, a real top derby match, Leeds versus Hunslet. Games didn't come any bigger than this. Hunslet, of course, is a suburb of Leeds to the south of the city. It was the industrial heart of the city with all the huge engineering works situated there. The Yorkshire saying of 'Where there's muck, there's money,' was very true. Unfortunately the money didn't go to the hundreds of families living amongst the grime and foundry waste in street after street of back to back houses that formed this breeding ground of truly great rugby league footballers. Hunslet's super homespun ground was Parkside, the graveyard for big clubs in cup ties. 'Posh' Leeds the Hunslet lads called the men from Headingley, and there was nothing that Hunslet teams liked better than to beat Posh Leeds, home or away.

Arthur had played in the Aussie derby games but none burned with such passion as the Leeds v Hunslet battles. The war song of the Parksiders was an old naval song, *We've swept the seas before Boys and so we shall again* and it rang out loud and clear whenever Hunslet took the lead against, or beat, Leeds. The crowds flocked to these games knowing there would be a match that held everything good and bad regarding rugby league in it. The Hunslet colours were recognisable anywhere. They were unique, myrtle, flame and white. The austere post war atmosphere meant those famous colours were not available. The Hunslet club did as others had to do for a season or two until times were better and adapted their strip, playing in green and white hooped jerseys with white shorts.

The Leeds coach, Frank Dolly Dawson was a legendary former Hunslet forward; he had been a tough, uncompromising player and a man who took his playing characteristics into coaching. The draw had given Leeds home advantage and everyone knew that the Hunslet side would put their bodies on the line rather than loose at Leeds. Headingley was packed solid for this dream cup tie. Estimates said the crowd was between 30,000 and 35,000. Leeds went with the side that did so well against Barrow: Cook; Cornelius, Price, T.L. Williams, Whitehead; Dickie Williams, Jenkins; Prosser, Murphy, Brereton, Clues, Watson and Owens. Hunslet, as one expected, had a larger number of local born lads in their side, which was: Bernard Lorriman;

Ted Carroll, 'Tuss' Griffiths, Sid Rookes, Freddie Williamson; Ernest Ruston, Frank Watson; Sam Newbound, Joe Britton, Gwynn Gronow, Doug Billings, Bill Metcalf and Des Clarkson.

The pitch had no time in which to recover from the pounding of the two Barrow games. Fortunately, as it was still freezing at night ground staff had chance to roll it early in the morning to at least offer a flat playing surface, although it was still terribly heavy and cut up as soon as play began. Again coach Dawson's plans were plain to see. His strong forwards set up attacks for the crafty Dai Jenkins and the speedy Dickie Williams to create space for the football craft of T.L. Williams and Gareth Price. Tommy Cornelius and Ernie Whitehead finished off the attacks. From these positions the opposition dare not give away penalties, for Leeds had a deadly marksman in Bert Cook who hardly ever missed a kick at goal. Arthur was soon greeted in the traditional newcomer-to-a-derby-match way. That is, he received a smack on the chin from the superb footballer, Des Clarkson. Again the ground would not allow fast, open rugby but what was on offer was an intriguing tactical battle amongst the forwards, each pack attempting to find a weakness in the other. The half backs, Williams and Jenkins for Leeds and Ruston and Watson for Hunslet, were perched like vultures, waiting for the half break by their forwards to enable them to swoop onto a pass and bring their backs into play. But so tight were both teams' defences that neither was able to create a chink in the other's armour.

Suddenly, out of the blue, there came a touch of genius that turned the game. The genius came from the number six for Leeds with ginger hair. Playing towards the 'ginnel' end, towards today's electric scoreboard, Arthur had a tilt up the South Stand touch line. From his play the ball, Dickie Williams gained possession around 30 yards out and set off on an arched run, towards the cricket ground corner. He beat three would be tacklers to dive triumphantly over the line about 10 yards in from the corner flag. Bert Cook landed a superb conversion to give a score of 5–0 to Leeds.

Hunslet, the 1946 beaten semi-finalists, would not give in. Wingman Freddie Williamson was hurled back from the line by Alf Watson, forward Des Clarkson was pulled back from over the Leeds try line by Prosser and Clues and Newbound was almost in at the corner. With both teams going at it hammer and tongs it was not surprising that frustration set in and Britton and Clues were warned about their actions in one set-to which had the Hunslet supporters howling for Arthur's dismissal. Then Clues and Clarkson had a set to, followed by Clues and Britton again. But this game missed the Clues-Ken Traill vendettas that went on for many years as Traill was left out of the Hunslet side on this occasion. These two great players clashed many times in their long careers, neither ever gaining the upper hand. The final whistle ended this ultra tough cup tie with Leeds marching on courtesy of Dickie Williams' brilliant try and Bert Cook's fine conversion. The score of 5–0 showed how close this contest was. Again the state of the sodden pitch contributed to the closeness of the game as it had in the previous round. Leeds now had the toughest of matches against the mighty Wigan at Central Park in round three.

Another huge crowd, another mud bound pitch and another close game was waiting for Leeds at Central Park as the Leeds selectors decided to keep the same team that had done so well in the previous two rounds. Arthur would have been pleased to see his former 'friends' from the test series, Ken Gee and Joe Egan, in the Wigan front row. No doubt he would have said, 'How Do' at some time during the game. Wigan were a star studded team amongst whom were Martin

Ryan, Jackie Cunliff, Ernie Ashcroft, Brian Nordgren, Johnny Lawrenson, Cec Mountford, Tommy Bradshaw, Frank Barton, Ted Ward and Billy Blan. The speedsters of Wigan, Nordgren and Lawrenson were slowed down considerably by the ankle deep mud as the Wigan pitch was in a worse condition than the Headingley pitch. Gee, Egan and Banks, the Wigan front row, decided to use roughhouse tactics early on but found Prosser, Brereton and Clues were willing opponents. Dickie Williams broke the deadlock when he sliced between Mountford and Ashcroft and found T.L. Williams in support. He, in turn, went through to Ryan and found Gareth Price on his shoulder. Les Williams put Price over to give Leeds a well deserved 3–0 lead.

Again because of the diabolical conditions, play was concentrated between the two 25 lines as the packs strove to beat both the mud and their opponents. Gee was playing on ground that suited him and stormed through twice only to have to wait for his support and the chances went begging. Then an incident occurred that has entered Leeds RLFC folklore. Taking a kick at goal under the posts in these conditions could not be classed as a certainty but as Wigan were penalised some 40 yards out from their own line and at an angle to the posts, Bert Cook came forward to tell the referee that he was kicking at goal. The crowd fell silent, apart from the hecklers who questioned Cooks mental state to be attempting such an impossible kick. Cook teed the ball up on a pile of mud, carefully measured out his run, and amid utter silence, ran up and with perfect timing and copy book follow through, hit this kick as sweet as any he hit before or to the end of his playing days. Bang, the ball flew the 40 yards, straight as a die to zoom over the crossbar a good 10 feet above it and plumb in the middle of the posts. People in Leeds claim to have heard the cheer that arose from Central Park at the instant the ball crossed between the posts. It took

Leeds to a 5–0 lead and even if Wigan scored a try, they had to convert it to stop Leeds from winning. The first man to congratulate Cook was his big mate, Arthur Clues, who with Dai Prosser, Chris Brereton, Ike Owens and Alf Watson, along with Con Murphy beating Joe Egan for the ball in the set scrums, laid the foundation for this memorable victory which put Leeds into the semi-final of the Challenge Cup.

But thoughts of the semi-final had to be put on the backburner as a hectic period of games fell over Easter. Hunslet came to Headingley on 4th April and turned in another brave performance as Leeds won by 5–2. These games provided great experience for the young Arthur Clues. The nail-biter continued the next day, Easter Saturday, when Leeds went to Mount Pleasant, Batley. There the 'Gallant Youths' lived up to their name and were narrowly beaten by Leeds, 3–0. Easter Monday had Leeds travelling 'Down't lane' to Castleford and another bruising confrontation to come away with a hard earned 10–2 win. The following day, Bramley visited Headingley and Leeds, playing their fourth game in five days, won this second 'derby' game 20–3. Four days later Leeds travelled to Swinton's Station Road to play the Lions and Leeds won 23–7. Arthur played in four of these five matches missing only the game at Castleford. He scored his first two tries for Leeds with a cracking pair in the team's win at Swinton.

On 19th April, Leeds took the last step towards a Wembley Cup final appearance when they met the holders of the cup, Wakefield Trinity, at Fartown, Huddersfield in the semi-final. It was the day before my 11th birthday and my dad took my pal and me to see the game. It was a brilliantly sunny day and Leeds served up a superb display of attacking rugby and excellent defence against a Trinity side that included Billy Teall, Ronnie Rylance, Billy Stott, Herbert Goodfellow, Len

Marson, Harry Wilkinson, Len Bratley and Denis Baddeley. Wakefield had beaten Wigan the year before and were a great cup fighting team. Leeds, again tackling like demons, showed just how good they could be carrying the ball by scoring 21 points. Tries came from Dickie Williams, Bert Cook, Chris Brereton, Ike Owens and Ernie Whitehead plus three goals by Cook to Trinity's nil. This result brought a record to Headingley as the only team to have gone to Wembley and have no points scored against them in any round.

Leeds returned to league football with one more game before the Wembley cup final. This was to play Hull Kingston Rovers at Craven Park, Hull. They beat the team by 22–6. Coach Frank Dawson, with one eye on the following week's Wembley game, rested Dickie Williams and Alf Watson. Bob Batten came in at stand off and Reg Wheatley packed down with Arthur in the second row. Otherwise Leeds played at full strength. Leeds were handily placed for a top four spot too as they had seven games remaining after the cup final. It was the final against the strong Bradford Northern side that was on the mind of the Leeds coach and players. Both teams travelled down to London on the Thursday of cup final week. Leeds' tactics were to use their big, mobile pack in a series of short passing moves, using Chris Brereton's outstanding ball playing as the key man in the forwards thrusts. Con Murphy was to work the dummy half position with Dai Prosser and Alf Watson either side of Brereton. Then Ike Owens and Arthur were to play outside of Prosser and Watson, giving a 'V' shape of support play amongst the forwards. Bradford on the other hand intended to use their swift handling half backs (Willie Davies and Donald Ward) each as an alternate dummy half. They also planned to use wide passing to run the big Leeds forwards and to sap their stamina. Indeed this is what they practised at their Westcliffe-on-Sea pre match HQ.

Bradford, so the story goes, had a problem on their

journey to the Stadium in that their coach driver managed to get hopelessly lost in London. Come the moment, come the man as big Frank Whitcombe squeezed his bulk behind the wheel and drove the team coach into the stadium. By all accounts big Frank held a heavy goods licence and had gained experienced in driving such vehicles during his war service.

Nearly 78,000 spectators crammed into the Wembley Stadium to witness this all Yorkshire final and the teams lined up at full strength. Leeds fielded: Cook; Cornelius, Price, T.L. Williams, Whitehead; Dickie Williams, Jenkins; Brereton, Murphy, Prosser, Clues, Watson and Owens. Bradford had experience and pace throughout their side and fielded: George Carmichael; Eric Batten, Jack Kitching, Ernest Ward, Emlyn Walters; Willie Davies, Donald Ward; Frank Whitcombe, Vic Darlison, Herbert Smith, Barry Tyler, Trevor Foster and Hagan Evans. The referee was the experienced Mr P. Cowell [Warrington]. Leeds had on their lucky tangerine jerseys with blue shorts and Bradford wore their traditional all white strip with the three red, amber and black bands around the chest and arms.

Bradford took the early exchanges as Walters was given two chances but could not outsmart the tight Leeds defence. Arthur was prominent in defence as Bradford's plan of running the Leeds pack around was paying off. But it was the trusty right boot of Bert Cook that gave the lead to Leeds when he landed a neat penalty goal on the half hour and that's how the half ended. Recognised as a good attacking side and with the excellent centre pairing of Kitching and Ward to run off the superb prompting of Willie Davies, Bradford found what no other side had found in the competition to date, that was a gap in the Leeds' defence. A brilliant pass by Donald Ward had Davies slicing through from about 40 yards out. Davies linked with his support and after a superb round of passing, Kitching found Ernest Ward who in turn sent

Walters haring over for Bradford's first try. Cook again put Leeds in the lead with another good penalty goal. This advantage was short lived as Ernest Ward showed his football prowess by dropping a great goal to give Northern a 5–4 lead. Arthur made a good break to get Price looping through the Northern cover but Cornelius was tackled into touch and the chance was lost. A kicking dual developed between Carmichael and Cook, which was a tactical feature of the game then. Surrounded by opposing forwards neither full back dare make a mistake for to do so would certainly result in a try to the opposition. Carmichael sent a spiralling punt up field to Cook who was faced by the Bradford second rower, Trevor Foster. Cook misjudged the spiral and dropped the ball. Then, giving Foster further advantage, slipped on the lush turf and fell down. Stood onside, Foster simply picked up the dropped ball and almost walked the 15 yards to the line for the winning try. In all fairness, although only four points separated the teams, Leeds had not been allowed to play their normal game as Bradford had tackled everything that moved and had been the better side with the ball.

Beaten by 8–4 the usual rumours surrounded the Leeds side. The talk was of a huge fall out between Dai Jenkins and Ike Owens on the eve of the game and that Gareth Price had crossed swords with Chris Brereton on the morning of the match. But the sad truth for Arthur was that his first, and as it cruelly turned out, his last Wembley appearance was with a well beaten side. Life goes on though and come the following Wednesday, three days after the final, Leeds went up the hill to the Barley Mow to play Bramley and won 26–7, Arthur scoring a 50 yard try.

Keighley visited Headingley on 10th May and again Leeds won by 43–10 but Arthur took a well earned rest. The Leeds pack was, Prosser, Cliff Carter, Ken Jubb, Watson, Reg Wheatley and Owens.

On 14th May, Barrow came again to Headingley. The Barrow team must have been sick of seeing the place and Leeds played their cup final team with Arthur back in the second row to record a hard fought win by 16–12. The next game on Wednesday 21st May was against the cup holders, Bradford Northern and a gate of over 40,000 squeezed into Headingley (me included), to see a brutally played affair with plenty of 'pay backs' from both sides in a pulsating 2–2 draw. Leeds had Walt Best on the wing for Ernie Whitehead, Bob Batten at stand off for the injured Dickie Williams and the excellent Jim Tynan at scrum half for Dai Jenkins. Arthur had put himself about in the type of match he loved and had clashed with several of the recent tourists as he looked for revenge for the Wembley defeat.

The next Leeds fixtures were against Featherstone Rovers, at home and away. On Saturday 24th May the game was at Headingley and Featherstone inflicted a surprise win by 17–14, Arthur scoring two good tries. The following Monday 26th May, Leeds went to Post Office Road to play Featherstone again and this time had a resounding win by 35–5, Arthur crossing the Rovers' line again for two great tries, one on a break from the half way line.

Saturday 31st May brought an end to the league season with a trip across Leeds to the home of Hunslet, Parkside. Leeds won a high scoring game by 30–22. This win cemented their place in the top four play off for the Championship. Unfortunately it meant that they had to travel to play the hardest team to beat in the whole league at that time, Wigan, at the majestic Central Park. This time as opposed to the cup tie, the ground was firm and the game was played at a furious pace with Wigan winning the day with a 21–11 victory. Arthur again fronted up to Ken Gee and Joe Egan on several occasions and scored one of Leeds' tries. The Leeds team on that final day of their season was: Cook; Bob Batten, Price,

T.L. Williams, Cornelius; Dickie Williams, Jenkins; Brereton, Murphy, Wheatley, Clues, Ike Owens in the second row and Alf Watson at loose forward.

Arthur had missed only one of the 21 games played by Leeds since his arrival and scored eight tries. Only Alf Watson with 10 tries was a higher scoring forward and Alf had played virtually all season which for Alf was 40 games. Ike Owens scored six tries in 30 games. So as Arthur's first half season ended, the Leeds public knew the club had signed someone very special. At the time there was a treat for the kids at our school as Ernie Whitehead, the Leeds wingman, worked in the office at Jonas Woodhead's Spring Works, on Kirkstall Road which ran at the bottom of our school street. Ernie lived quite near to our school and walked each day past us to go home for lunch. I plucked up enough courage one particular lunchtime to ask if he would show us his Wembley medal. On his return trip he came over to me and produced the gold medal. He let a few of us hold it and read the inscription on the back: 'E. Whitehead, Runners Up, 1946' it read. It was a beautiful gold medal with the four shields superimposed on the front – wonderful!

3

CRICKET AND ANOTHER RUGBY LEAGUE CUP FINAL

Arthur moved during the summer from the 13-a-side game to 11-a-side as he swapped the shoulder pads and shin guards of rugby league for the pads and gloves of cricket. His team was the Leeds Cricket Club who played to a very high standard in the Yorkshire Council and whose home ground was the test venue at Headingley. The level of cricket was only one step away from county cricket and the weekend running around on the oval kept him in reasonable fitness.

The 1947–1948 rugby league season started for Leeds with a trip to Fartown to take on the very strong Huddersfield side. The opposition boasted the inclusion of Arthur's Australian test team mate Lionel Cooper, his other mate from Australia the excellent full back Johnny Hunter, plus the master international footballer, Pat Devery. An acceptable 6–6 draw was the result but the following Wednesday brought a 20–8 defeat at Odsal. This brought the Leeds players down to earth. Arthur scored one of the tries against Bradford Northern when Leeds put out a most unusual pack compared to the previous season of Wheatley, Horsfall, Newbound, Hulme, Clues and Des Foreman (Des scored the other try at Odsal) with Bert Cook kicking one goal. The next game brought a disastrous defeat for Leeds when Huddersfield won 32–18. This was one of the 10 games Arthur missed that season because of various small injuries. This defeat was followed by a terrific win at the Boulevard where Leeds beat

Hull FC 13–10 with Arthur crossing the line for one of the Leeds tries. Keighley were defeated at Lawkholme Lane 14–13, Arthur crossing again for a good try.

The Yorkshire Cup began with a very difficult first round two legged tie against the old enemy, Bradford Northern. The first leg was at Headingley on 13th September and the Leeds side was: Jack Kelly; Bob Batten, Gareth Price, Denis Warrior, Tommy Cornelius, Ernie Whitehead; Dickie Williams, Dai Jenkins; Reg Wheatley, Cliff Carter, Jack Newbound, Des Foreman, Joe Flanagan and Arthur Clues. It was a strange looking team in September compared to the Wembley side the previous May but never-the-less the team achieved a great win of 11–5 with Des Foreman scoring two good tries and Arthur ploughing through the Northern tacklers for another. Jack Kelly added one goal.

Their tails up now, Leeds next took on Keighley at home and won a crushing 40–10 victory. Des Foreman (in fine form) and Arthur scored one try apiece. Reg Wheatley scored a cracking hat trick of tries for a prop forward with Joe Flanagan and Cliff Carter each scoring to make it a forward's day out.

The 24th September was the big day as Leeds defended a lead of six points in the second leg of the Yorkshire Cup against Bradford at Odsal. One or two enforced changes took place in the side which was: Kelly; Batten, Price, Cornelius, Whitehead; Dickie Williams, Jenkins; Wheatley, Carter, Chris Brereton, Foreman, Flanagan and Clues. In a titanic struggle, Bradford won the game 11–9, giving Leeds an aggregate win of 20–16 and a passage into round two.

In the league, Wakefield Trinity was beaten at Belle Vue by 38–12, Foreman scoring a try again. On 1st October, Dewsbury visited Headingley in round two of the Yorkshire Cup. Cornelius was at full back, with Denis Warrior returning to the centres and a back three in the pack of Clues, Flanagan and Ike Owens. Flanagan, Price and Owens scored tries and

Whitehead kicked three goals to go into the County Cup semi-final against Castleford at Headingley on 15th October.

In between the cup ties, Hull Kingston Rovers beat Leeds in Hull by 23–3 and Leeds beat Featherstone Rovers at home by 27–6. This game saw the debut of Len Kenny who, like Arthur, had joined Leeds from his native Australia. Len, who was a great crowd pleaser, went on to score 22 tries for Leeds in his first season and finished as top try scorer. After the Dewsbury cup game Arthur missed five matches but Cook returned at full back for the semi-final when the Leeds pack was, Prosser, Carter, Wheatley, Foreman, Flanagan and Owens. Dickie Williams, Owens and Cook scored tries and Whitehead (4) and Foreman (1) kicked the goals in a 19–4 win which took Leeds into the final of the Yorkshire Cup. Their opponents were Wakefield Trinity whom Leeds had beaten convincingly both in last season's Challenge Cup semi-final and this season's league game at Belle Vue. Trinity had just signed the young Australian player Dennis Booker and he was to play for them in the County Cup Final having had only one game in Trinity's colours before the big game.

Before the final, the Leeds team were well beaten at Wilderspool by Warrington 38–13, but they pulled back the following week with a 24–12 win over Halifax.

The County Cup final day was played on 1st November at Fartown, Huddersfield before a crowd of 24,344. On their way to the final, Trinity had beaten Hull Kingston Rovers in the two legged first round, Hull FC in round two and Huddersfield in the semi-final. The two teams were, Wakefield Trinity: W. Teall; J. Perry, W. Stott, D. Booker, R. Jenkinson; A. Fletcher, H. Goodfellow; H. Wilkinson, L. Marson, J. Higgins, H. Murphy, J. Booth and L. Bratley. Leeds: J. Kelly; D. Warrior, B. Cook, G. Price, E. Whitehead; Dickie Williams, D. Jenkins; D. Prosser, C. Carter, R. Wheatley, A. Clues, J. Flanagan and I. Owens. Stott kicked a penalty goal to send Trinity in at half time 2–0 up. A clever

Goodfellow try and a Stott conversion took Wakefield clear by 7–0 but Whitehead kicked a neat penalty goal to bring a strangely subdued Leeds back into the game and a brilliant passing movement had Dickie Williams rounding Billy Teall to score a crucial try. Whitehead coolly slotted over the conversion and it was 7 points all. That is how the game finished.

The replay was four days later on Wednesday, 5th November, Guy Fawkes night, at Odsal Stadium. And there were some fireworks alright. Leeds made one change; Chris Brereton replaced the injured Reg Wheatley at blind side prop. Trinity were without Billy Stott their great captain and leader. Reg Jenkinson moved to the centre and Ronnie Rylance took Jenkinson's spot on the wing and also took over as captain. A total of 32,000 people were off work (allegedly at their grandma's funeral) that afternoon as the Leeds pack came to grips with the Trinity six. The two tough men, Arthur and Len Bratley, knocked lumps off each other as Jackie Perry kicked a penalty goal to give Trinity the lead but minutes later Cook dropped a goal to level the scores. Arthur took revenge on Harry Murphy for a previous incident then a mistake at the scrum allowed Harry Wilkinson to barge over for a try and soon after Len Bratley scored the easiest of tries when he fielded a poor clearing kick by Leeds. The score was 8–2 to Trinity and they were hanging on for a gallant win when Price intercepted a wayward pass and drew Billy Teall to send Joe Flanagan in. Whitehead converted to make it 8–7. There was virtually nothing between these teams over 160 minutes of football but Trinity hearts missed a beat when Wakefield were penalised under their own posts. Ernie Whitehead teed up the kick to bring the old cup to Headingley. The huge crowd went silent as Ernie slowly walked back on his measured run. He had been kicking brilliantly since taking over from the usual kickers Cook and Kelly (both kickers were injured earlier that season). It was a simple kick, and as he strode forward he struck the ball well but it swung wide and the chance was gone. Wakefield had gained ample revenge for the heavy semi-final defeat the previous season as well as the home loss in the league only seven weeks before. Arthur had lost another cup final with Leeds. It seemed to him that he was way out of luck.

Leeds beat Leigh 36–16 in the next home game after the Yorkshire Cup Final. Next was another big game as Leeds played the touring Kiwis on 12th November. Several changes were made to host this prestigious game and the team was: Cook; Kenny, Warrior, T.L. Williams, Whitehead; Downes, Tynan; Prosser, Davies, Brereton, Clues, Foreman and Owens. Arthur romped over for a crackerjack of a try, the little chip, re-gather, side step of the full back and a sprint over. Len Kenny, Ernie Whitehead and Chris Brereton added tries and Whitehead kicked two goals.

At this time another signing was rumoured in the newspaper. Leeds declared interest in the Queensland Rugby League utility back, Ted Verrenkamp. It was just a whisper at the time, enough to tickle interest, without saying too much. At this time, Arthur was helping out on the ground staff at Headingley and Bert Cook worked behind the mixer for the Leeds Chairman, Sir Edwin Airy, who had a building business in Woodhouse Lane, opposite what is now the Engineering Block of Leeds University. Both overseas players were in digs directly opposite the gates to the cricket ground in Headingley on Escourt Avenue. The landlady was called Alice Burns and all the players who stayed there thought the world of her.

Leigh beat Leeds at Hilton Park 11–10 and then Arthur had a particularly good game against Dewsbury at home when the men from Crown Flatt were beaten 29–5. Arthur scored Leeds' only try in a hard fought win by 7–5 at the old Barley Mow as the Bramley side gave 'big brother' a fright.

Following this came double defeats for Leeds as Hull FC beat them at Headingley, 11–7 and Hunslet had a 13–3 win over their old enemy at Parkside. From the start of the season Arthur had missed five of the first 15 games. He also missed the Hunslet game but returned the week after to play in a fine 17 game uninterrupted run.

The Christmas period brought the usual three games in three days, starting with Batley at Mount Pleasant on 25th December which gave Leeds a 13–4 win. Wakefield Trinity came to Leeds on 26th December and were beaten by 31–0. Arthur crashed over the line for a strong try and Len Kenny recorded a hat trick of tries. The 27th December saw Batley play the return from Christmas Day and Kenny scored another hat trick (two in two days) in the 31–5 win. January 1948 started badly for Leeds as they lost three games on the trot. They lost to Halifax away at Thrum Hall 5–2, Wigan at home 11–9 and Dewsbury away at Crown Flatt 7–2. Then Leeds beat York at Clarence Street 17–5.

The Leeds faithful were given a January treat with the debut of Ted Verrenkamp playing for Leeds against Oldham at Headingley. I can remember seeing him arrive at the ground along with Arthur and thinking to myself how small and lightweight he looked. My, did he play above his weight. The team that day was: Cook; Warrior, Price, Cornelius, Whitehead; Ted Verrenkamp and Jenkins; Prosser, Davies, Wheatley, Clues, Flanagan and Owens and in the 26–5 win, Arthur raced in for his eighth try of the season. Verrenkamp had an excellent debut, tackling like a tiger and running and creating for his centres very well indeed.

Around this time, Harry Bath who had firstly joined Barrow as a great signing, then fairly quickly moved south to Warrington and there teamed up with Arthur in representative football to form arguably the best second row partnership ever seen in this country. But the new kid on the block was Ted Verrenkamp. Although he was a little on the small side, Ted had a natural long running stride which gave him the appearance of bounding, Kangaroo like. With the already settled in pair of Arthur and Bert Cook, Ted was not going to be the only new Australasian in digs at Escourt Avenue. Not too far down the track, Bob McMasters and Ken Kearney, the Wallaby prop and hooker would join Leeds and move in with Alice Burns. Ted told me about the three years without sleep that he endured in these digs. Arthur and Bert Cook had the bedroom above Ted; he reckoned that the two blokes above him were the noisiest pair in the world. They were forever up to something that involved noise and banging about. Ted had played against Arthur when he represented Queensland against New South Wales and had met Arthur's aggression at first hand on the field. Arthur's first advice to Ted when he arrived in the digs was, 'Never show these pommy bastards that you are hurt or they will maul you and eat you.' Arthur had a full sized human dummy in his cupboard that he used to hang his suit on. To illustrate his point, he would get out the dummy and show Ted the relative pressure attack if a tackler was coming on rough. 'Hit the bastards here Eddie,' he would advise him, showing the area to attack, 'If he squeals, give it to him again.'

But Ted Verrenkamp's over riding memory was of Arthur saying to him, 'Did you see who it was that caught you Eddie?' This was as the blood oozed from a facial hit.

'Yes, it was number eight from their side,' replied Ted.

Arthur waited his time then flattened the aggressor and said, 'All square Eddie.'

Ted recalled one game at Castleford when two big colliers had given it to Arthur all the match and in the last few minutes tackled him, two on one, and were gouging his eyes and squeezing his private parts. Arthur never flinched and as the gouger's fingers slipped from his eyes down his cheek, Arthur's big teeth closed like a vice on the gouger's fingers. The gouger screamed like a pig and shouted to the referee that Arthur had bitten his hand, the experienced referee simply said, 'What were your fingers doing in his mouth anyway? Play on.'

After the game, Arthur was having a cup of tea in the player's room when the same big collier came in and made straight for him. Arthur stopped him dead in his tracks when he said, 'Look, the game's over and you will have a chance to get your own back next time we play opposite each other.' The huge Castleford lad saw the sense in that but Arthur finished off with, 'I will give you a good piece of advice though. Don't put so much salt and vinegar on your fish and chips next time. I could taste the bloody stuff when your hand was in my mouth.' Arthur was a devil, according to Ted. He told me, 'When Ken Kearney moved in with me at number 14 the four of us, Ken, Arthur, Bert and myself had some high old times'.

Arthur was 'Jack the Lad' in the digs, getting up to all sorts but always had enough respect for Alice Burns never to go too far. As Ted Verrenkamp explained, 'He had a favourite trick which he played regularly on dear Alice. As we all sat waiting to be served at the dinner table, Alice would swish past in her long skirt with warm, long, woollen socks on her feet. Arthur would just lift the hem of her skirt, only an inch, and with that heavy Aussie accent of his would say, "Alice sweetheart, you've put those passion killers on again. You know what it does to me!" All the players had a laugh and Alice always hit Arthur across his ears and had a good laugh herself at his antics. They were very happy and enjoyable days at Headingley then.'

Ted related a rather nice poignant little tale that involved Arthur, Bert, Ken and Bob McMasters (all sadly passed away now). To get to training on the cold winter evenings from Escourt Avenue to the football ground dressing rooms, the players had to walk down to Headingley Lane, turn left onto Cardigan Road, turn right down to St Michaels lane, turn right again and walk the 300 yards into the ground. With Arthur, Ted and Ken working on the ground staff they took the same walk every working day. Directly across the road from their digs was the main cricket ground gate. Through that gate and 300 yards away were the dressing rooms. Ted asked the secretary if they could borrow the big gate key so that it would cut down walking time to work and training by 10 minutes. The secretary agreed and lent them the key. According to Ted, he kept this borrowed key even when he returned home to Australia. He hung the key on a hook on one of his shelves in his kitchen in Queensland in remembrance of his happy years at the glorious Headingley and it is still there to this day.

Arthur had warned Ted of the language difference between Australia and Leeds. He told Ted that after only being in Leeds a day or so, he asked the secretary how he could get into the city centre. 'It's easy, walk up to Cardigan Road, only a matter of a couple of hundred yards and jump on a tram. All the trams go into City Square, in the middle of Leeds,' said the secretary.

Arthur waited a few moments for a tram, jumped on and sat down by the platform. 'City Centre, please,' Arthur said to the clippie (a man with the tramways hat perched on the back of his head).

'A penny love,' said the conductor in that peculiar Leeds vernacular. Arthur had never been called 'love' by a man before and kept a sharp eye on the clippie. He clenched his fist ready should he be approached. It unnerved Arthur for a while until he realised it was a general term of endearment used by most Loiners.

The game after Verrenkamp's debut was a tough one, albeit at Headingley, to take on 'The Wire', the rough Warrington outfit with Arthur's old mate Harry Bath leading their pack. Changes in the Leeds team saw Denis Warrior move out to the wing for the injured Len Kenny and Tommy Cornelius take Warrior's place in the centre. Bath had a great game for Warrington but was matched all the way by Arthur. People who witnessed these two fine exponents of forward play competing against each other agreed that together they would make an outstanding partnership. They had of course done that in Australia where, without a doubt, the Aussies second row against England in 1946 would have been Clues and Bath had Harry not been injured. The game, Leeds v Warrington ended as a 5–5 draw when Dai Jenkins slid over for the Leeds try and Ernie Whitehead kicked a goal.

The Challenge Cup first round, first leg, was against York at Leeds and began with a sound win over the Minster Men by 23–9. The second leg was at Clarence Street and was won 13–0. Arthur added another great try in the home leg win. Two weeks later, round two of the Challenge Cup took Leeds to a tough game at Central Park to play the mighty Wigan. A 17–3 defeat ended Leeds' Challenge Cup hopes for that particular season. Worse was to come when a week later, Leeds had to return to Central Park in the league game. This time Leeds were trounced by 41–6 as Wigan ran riot in a barnstorming display. Leeds made several changes from the team that had played the previous week in this heavy defeat with T.L. Williams at full back, Bob Batten on the wing, Jim Tynan at scrum half and Maurice Ogden at hooker.

One week after the big defeat at Wigan, Leeds introduced another overseas signing. He was Jack Pansegrouw, a South African Rugby Union giant. Despite his 6 foot 5 inch height and 19 stone frame, he was a very amiable guy. He always had a smile and a cheery word. He made his debut against York in the league game at Headingley, a game that Leeds won 46–2. In this game, Arthur partnered big Jack in the second row, who went in for another try from about 30 yards out. After the whistle had sounded the end of this game, all those in the schoolboys' enclosure, ran onto the field to welcome the big

South African. He was happy to have been promoted to the Leeds first team and pleased with the winning result. As I slapped him on the waist (his back was too high for me to reach), he turned, scooped me up and sat me on his shoulders. He walked all the way to the ramp up to the dressing room with me perched up there. On Monday evening I was proud as punch to be in a photograph on the back page of the *Yorkshire Evening News*, being carried off by big Jack Pansegrouw.

Jack didn't play very long at Leeds. He soon went to Halifax and played in their second row in the 1949 Wembley cup final against Bradford Northern which Bradford won 12–0.

For Leeds, a defeat by Castleford at Wheldon Road by 18–5 was followed by five consecutive wins. The wins were against: Featherstone Rovers at Post Office Road (20–9); Castleford at home (9–0) (Arthur scored another try in this game); Bramley at home (21 to 16); Hunslet at home (12–0); and Hull Kingston Rovers at home (29–12). Leeds lost their two final league games, both away at Oldham and Bradford Northern 12–5 and 9–3 respectively.

As the season ended it was obvious that most of the great pack of forwards and some of the backs that had carried the team to Wembley in 1947 were 'getting old together'. Dai Prosser had played before the war, Chris Brereton was getting to the back end of his career and Con Murphy had retired with the magnificent Alf Watson. Ike Owens too had seen quite a lot of action and like other great players, the war years had interrupted what, even then, had been a wonderful career. Reg Wheatley, that grand servant of the Leeds club who had been a prisoner of war in Europe for a few years, moved to Leigh. Dai Jenkins had played with Con Murphy for Acton and Willesden, then Streatham and Mitcham, both London clubs, well before the war. Ernie Whitehead, and T.L. Williams could not be considered long term prospects and Jack Kelly was allowed to leave the club after a good few years of top class service. Gareth Price, a superb centre, joined Halifax and captained the Thrum Hall side in the 1949 cup final. That left Arthur, Dickie Williams and Bert Cook of the 'old guard'. A decent team could still be built around these three mainstays. Arthur was still only 23 years old and developing quickly into a tremendous back row forward but he needed support if his outstanding work from the second row was to be best served. Dickie would have been around 26 and still a very good stand off half. Bert was about the same age as Dickie and although troubled by a long standing dislocated shoulder, was a good goal kicker and prepared to soldier on. There was time for these three to weld a squad together. Arthur had scored 11 tries in the 1947–1948 season and had created many more with his strong running and clever ball handling. Further representative honours were just around the corner.

4

BACK HOME,
BACK TO SCHOOL

Arthur took a trip back to Australia during the close season. Whilst on this trip he was introduced to the American film star and leading man, Richard Egan. The pair struck up a firm friendship that lasted many years and Richard attended several games at Headingley as Arthur's guest. At this time, Bert Cook accepted a job at the Leeds private school, Leeds City High School as head of physical education. His contact for the job was in fact the owner of the school, Mr Frank Wood. Mr Wood was also on the Leeds board of directors and was the company treasurer. Mr Wood's daughter Muriel was the school principle and held degrees from both Leeds and Cambridge Universities. Muriel later became Mrs Clues.

At a meeting on the eve of the 1948–1949 season, the Rugby Football League International Committee decided that, because of the avid interest in the game throughout the country, the defunct Other Nationalities side would be reinstated and be entered into the existing local tri-nations competition between England, Wales and France to make a four team international league. Selection for the new side was open to any player born anywhere other than in any of the other three countries. It was in these Other Nationalities teams that the partnership of Clues and Bath came to fruition.

Leeds started the season in a blaze of publicity by signing

two Australian Rugby Union international front row stars. The new signings were Ken 'Killer' Kearney, the powerful hooker and 'Wallaby' Bob McMaster the big prop forward who also became a professional wrestler in the UK. Big Bob was also a decent goal kicker. Another signing was the Oldham second row forward, Les Thomas. Thomas was the unofficial holder of the title of the 'fastest forward in the game'. He had the ability to score tries from long distances during a match. But the dual signing that held the most interest was the capture from the Scottish border's district of a young centre and wingman from the Hawick club, Tommy Wright and the flying Andrew Turnbull. A number of other players signed that season. These players included Ike Proctor the strong Maori centre or stand off half from Halifax as well as Des Clarkson the former Hunslet, Leigh and England loose forward (born and bred in Airedale, Castleford). Des was one of the smartest turned out footballers ever seen. A swap move between Leeds and Bramley saw the terrific servant Denis Warrior go to Bramley and two good players come to Headingley. These players were Aussie Bob Bartlett (a classical centre) and local Bramley lad, Denis Murphy. Denis was a utility forward, preferably a second row man.

The first game was at Headingley that season played against Bramley. The new look Leeds pack consisted of McMaster, Kearney, Newbound, Clues, Wheatley and Owens. Andrew Turnbull and Tommy Wright formed a right wing-right centre combination with Gareth Price and Denis Warrior on the left. Dickie Williams and Dai Jenkins were the half backs and Bert Cook played at full back. The result was a disappointing 7–7 draw. The bright spot was the great promise shown by the two young Scotts, Wright and Turnbull. Put clear by Wright on the half way line, Turnbull showed a remarkable turn of speed to race in for the first of many tries for Leeds. He had a career that earned the swift Scotsman one full cap against New Zealand in 1951 and a place on the 1954 tour to Australia and New Zealand.

Two away games came next. The first game at Leigh, saw Arthur and Newbound drop out through injury with Dai Prosser the old war horse coming in at open side prop and McMaster moving across to number 10. Les Thomas took Arthur's place in his debut in the second row. A close game was expected as usual at Hilton Park and Leigh won through 11–10. Hunslet won the second game 16–10 and although Arthur returned and scored a cracking 30 yard try, the Parksiders were well worthy of their win.

It was a bad start to the new season. The new players found it hard to gel, apart from the youthful Wright and Turnbull who looked a class apart. The tragically unlucky Wright had only a few more games at full fitness to show what a centre he would have been. Tommy Wright had played only 7 times for Leeds when he sustained a bad knee injury at Central Park, Wigan, on 25th September 1948. This was only his seventh outing as a professional player. He attempted a couple of come-backs playing a further 10 games but his knee was so bad that it forced his retirement and he returned to Scotland.

Leeds beat Keighley at home 21–15 with Arthur again showing his class by performing another long range, side stepping and swerving run. But the mediocre form of the Loiners continued as Bramley were victorious at the Barley Mow in a great 17–13 win for the 'Villagers'. Arthur was one for talking to the referees during a game and many times would conduct a running discussion over an incident that had recently happened. He'd ask the referee point blank, 'Are you f****** blind ref?'

Meanwhile players such as Charlie Appleton of

Warrington and Laurie Thorpe of Wakefield would smile and make comments such as, 'Just get on with your bloody game Arthur,' or, 'Keep them bloody tackles down and mind your bloody language.'

Young Wright had hurt his leg against Bramley and in the Yorkshire Cup first leg game against Halifax at home, Leeds took the unusual step of playing the speedy Ike Owens in the centre as partner to Andy Turnbull. Les Thomas took Owens' place at loose forward and Reg Wheatley moved from prop into the second row with Arthur. The first leg developed into a real cup tie with the tough Halifax pack making it hard work for the Leeds six in a very hard fought 10–10 draw. Tuesday 14th September saw the second leg at Thrum Hall played before a big crowd. This game was just as hard as the first leg. Denis Warrior took Ike Owens' first leg centre spot, Owens reverting back to number 13 and Thomas taking Wheatley's second row berth. It was a grinding battle with bouts of fisticuffs blowing up throughout the game. Warrior, Price and Owens scored tries and Cook landed one goal in a tough 11–5 win giving an aggregate win of 21–15 to the Loiners.

Four days later these two brutal cup ties showed in a slow Leeds performance against a strong Warrington side at Wilderspool. The Wire produced a top drawer show to beat Leeds 39–17. Although the Warrington half backs, Fleming and Helme had great games, the Leeds paring of Ted Verrenkamp at stand off and Johnny Feather, the excellent local lad at scrum half, matched them. Les Thomas showed his versatility by playing in the centre for the injured Warrior. Arthur and Harry Bath, despite having a great understanding when playing together, could never be mates when in opposition. Both gave as much as they received in this latest game, when they had several dust ups.

Dewsbury came to Headingley and young Wright attempted a come-back in the centre. He scored a nice try in the 17–5 win for Leeds. Wigan were the next opponents at Central Park as the miserable results continued and Wigan rubbed it in with a crushing 54–8 victory. Arthur had several rounds with Ken Gee and Joe Egan as usual but hard as he tried to stop the Wigan steamroller attack it was impossible to hold them for long when they were in this mood. Games were being played on Saturdays and Wednesdays in September but the Yorkshire Cup second round against Hunslet at Headingley was played on the Thursday evening. Arthur's well taken try could not stop the Parksiders marching into the semi-final on the back of a 10–7 win.

Arthur, like all top players, wanted to win as many cups as possible in his playing career. Leeds' loss at the hands of Bradford Northern at Wembley in 1946 and then drawing and later losing to Wakefield Trinity in the Yorkshire Cup final were bitter pills to swallow. The defeat by Hunslet saw the transfer to Castleford of the great Ike Owens for £2,750 which was a record at the time. In a very short time Ike moved again to Huddersfield for exactly the same fee. He was a wonderful, quick and skilled forward and an excellent tackler.

Each time Leeds appeared to have a cup winning formula they seemed to perform badly on the main day. The lack of cup winning successes on Arthur's playing record speaks volumes for his playing ability as he gained a reputation as a great player solely on league performances rather than through many Wembley appearances or County Cup or Championship wins. The title of the best ever second row forward was earned in the week in week out bread and butter league games and by the words of his opponents. All Arthur's opponents agreed with the great Jim Lewthwaite of Barrow, who said earlier, 'You always wished that he was on your side.'

The board of directors must have looked worried as the dreadful run of results continued week after week. The supporters at Leeds had been brought up on success in the Challenge Cup, the County Cup and by high positions in the league. Up to now in the league their record was: played 8; won 2; drawn 1; and lost 5. This was not good enough at all for a club of Leeds' standing. Another factor always evident at Headingley was that to win was not the be all and end all of the matter. The Leeds team had to win well and play an exciting brand of open football. The fast exhilarating style of the pre war stars, Stanley Brogden, Stanley Smith, Eric Harris, Vic Hey, Frank O'Rourke, Fred Harris and Jeff Moores was still remembered and idolised and the supporters wanted those days back. The only real player of absolute star quality in the side was Arthur and he, of course, was a forward. Much as the Leeds faithful admired and loved Arthur they yearned to see the speedy wingmen being served by classy centres, fed in turn by an excellent stand off half. Dicky Williams had given wonderful service for several seasons but his term of office at Leeds was drawing to a close and whilst Wigan's Cec Mountford, Warrington's Jacky Fleming and Barrow's Willie Horne were still brilliant players, the Leeds public thought their star backs were waning. The Leeds fans looked on with envy at the likes of Lionel Cooper, Brian Bevan, Brian Nordgren, Jack McLean, Albert Johnson and Stan McCormick flying down the touch line. Although they now had Drew Turnbull playing, they yearned for more. The mediocre pace of Ernie Whitehead, Tommy Cornelius, Denis Warrior and Len Kenny (all good players) was nothing compared to the list above. The delicate situation at stand off was highlighted when one looked at the personnel who pulled on the number six jersey, Dickie Williams, Verrenkamp, Downes (from the A team) and Ike Proctor. In the Cup year of 1946 Dickie Williams missed only four games all season. In the 1948–1949 season he missed 18 games. Without Dickie at stand off half, Leeds struggled.

Fortunately results started to improve when Halifax came to Leeds in the next league game. Leeds beat Halifax 19–7 and Arthur had his best game of the season, showing all his skills off in a super display of second row play and making tries for young Downes and Johnny Feather.

Keighley were heavily beaten at Lawkholme 33–5. Then the strong Huddersfield side came to Headingley where Arthur produced another memorable game, chipping and catching then bursting clear. He shot over the line himself to bring the house down. He rounded Johnny Hunter, one of the safest tacklers around, stepped across the cover tackle of big Lionel Cooper and sent Drew Turnbull galloping over. Then, late in the game, he sent Les Thomas sprinting clear to score after Arthur had taken three Fartown players out and slipped Thomas a peach of a pass to run onto. This 17–10 win was followed by a tough tourist fixture as Leeds played the Australians on 27th October on a beautiful autumn Wednesday afternoon. Leeds could have won this game but threw away several clear-cut chances and were finally beaten by 15–2. A close 6–3 victory at Crown Flatt against a strong Dewsbury outfit eased things in the league and although Arthur played in this game, Leeds were soon to be without him for 12 weeks with a knee injury. Another 12–7 win at Batley meant that Leeds had won five league games on the trot from looking down and out. But the bubble burst the following week at Odsal when Northern battered a Leeds side without Arthur's strength and skill and gained a big 21–2 victory.

To cover for Arthur's long lay off, Leeds bought Des Clarkson from Leigh and Gwynn Gronow from Hunslet. Clarkson was an international loose forward and Gronow was a good footballer at prop. Leigh came to Headingley and won 9–5. Then on Christmas Day, Leeds beat Batley at Leeds 26–11 with debutant Des Clarkson scoring a try.

Leeds lost the next four league games: Wakefield Trinity 7–0 at Belle Vue; Warrington at Headingley 14–0 (a game that saw Ken Kearney play in the second row); Halifax at Thrum Hall 6–0; and Wigan at Leeds by 14–12. The supporters found it hard to accept the fact that Leeds had scored only 12 points in four games. There are few fans like the ones at Leeds. They have always been hungry for success and whilst many other clubs' supporters may accept the attitude that a win is a win, this doesn't apply to Leeds. They demand that their team wins well and regularly! Whitehaven were beaten 5–3 at Headingley but things were not going well without Arthur. Then came two games played on consecutive weekends that I personally remember vividly. The first game was played against Featherstone Rovers at the compact but atmospheric Post Office Road. On a dull, rainy late January afternoon Featherstone outplayed Leeds for most of the game. The Leeds side were: Cook; Turnbull, Ike Proctor, T.L. Williams, Verrenkamp; Dickie Williams, Jenkins; Gwynn, Gronow, Ken Kearney, Bob McMaster, Alan Kendrick, Thomas and Des Clarkson. The Leeds team had trouble containing the lively Rovers pack and half backs. I went to this game with my Dad and remember feeling down in the dumps as Leeds were trailing by 8–7 going into the final few minutes. Suddenly, with hardly any time left, the ball was switched to Gwynn Gronow who quickly but ever so sweetly dropped a goal from about 10 yards out, almost straight to give Leeds a one point win when all seemed lost. I went with my Dad the following week to the grand old Clarence Street ground at York, to watch York v Leeds. The extra goody here was Bob Bartlett's debut for Leeds. Bob was an excellent, classy centre. The Australian came originally to Bramley but Arthur and Ted Verrenkamp told the Leeds directors just how good this superb centre was. The Leeds directors struck a deal that brought Bartlett and Denis Murphy to Leeds and Denis

Warrior and a big fee went down Kirkstall Lane, across the River Aire and up the hill to the Barley Mow. The Leeds changes from the previous week were Bartlett and Price in the centre for Proctor and Les Williams, Proctor moved to stand off for Dickie Williams, young Downes was in at number seven for Jenkins. Dai Prosser was in at number eight for Gronow who moved to number 10 in place of McMaster. Denis Murphy made his debut in place of Les Thomas. It was another dull afternoon and one player who stood out for York in both attack and defence was a chap who was very thin on top – in fact he was quite bald. In the programme I found out his name mainly because he was such a good player. Years after I realised that he was that excellent servant to the York club for many years, Charlie Taylor. The game was deadlocked at 7–7, just like at Featherstone going into injury time. In the previous attack, the ball was transferred to Bert Cook who took a snap shot at a drop goal but was just wide with the attempt. Full time loomed and it was still 7–7 until the ball was thrown to Gwynn Gronow. He stood in an identical position to the previous week at Featherstone and produced the perfect drop goal again to give Leeds the points once more. Has a prop forward ever before or since dropped goals to win two consecutive matches? Gwynn Gronow did this in style.

Denis Murphy, the former Bramley second row forward was a good utility signing and played many times with Arthur in the second row. He also had fine games at loose forward, in the centre and even at full back and as stand in goal kicker. Denis also played in the Combined Services Rugby League XV in the famous match at Odsal on 29th April 1943 when a terrific team of servicemen from the Rugby League professional ranks took on and beat a Combined Services Rugby Union XV under Union rules. The war time rugby league team was, Lance-Corporal Ernest Ward [Bradford

Northern]; Sergeant-Instructor Roy Francis [Barrow], Leading Aircraftsman Johnny Lawrenson [Wigan], Corporal Jim Stott [St Helens], Corporal Alan Edwards [Salford]; Sergeant Stan Brogden [Hull FC], Bombardier Harry Royal [Dewsbury]; Sergeant-Instructor Dai Prosser [Leeds], Driver Les White [Hunslet], Lance-Corporal Chris Brereton [Halifax], Sergeant Denis Murphy [Bramley], Flight-Sergeant Emlyn Watkins [Wigan], Sergeant Ike Owens [Leeds], Sergeant Bill Chapman [Warrington] and Sergeant-Instructor Trevor Foster [Bradford Northern].

Batley were Leeds' opponents in the Challenge Cup first round. In the first leg at Headingley, Leeds won 16–2. In the second leg at Mount Pleasant, Leeds again won 7–4 giving an aggregate win of 23–6. Arthur made his return to the team when Leeds met Hull Kingston Rovers at Craven Park. Arthur had a quiet game in the 20–17 win. He had missed 13 games because of minor surgery to repair an old knee injury. The second round of the Challenge Cup took Hunslet to Headingley and Arthur was back to his best with an outstanding display in the 14–8 hard earned win. This gave the Leeds side their seventh consecutive success since the narrow defeat by Wigan on 8th January.

The tough journey to play the rugged Whitehaven ended in a game mirroring the journey. It was a tough, rugged encounter with Leeds making the long trip home defeated 12–2. Arthur had to miss this game after straining his groin in training. He was back though for the third round Challenge Cup tie at Headingley against the powerful Huddersfield side. Again Leeds were completely outplayed, outpaced and outgunned. The Fartowers went through to the semi-final on the strength of a stunning 20–9 win in front of a disillusioned Leeds crowd, only to loose to the strong Halifax team. The crowd let their feelings be known after the cup tie. Leeds next travelled to that cauldron of noise and unrelenting on field violence, the Boulevard. No place in the whole league was as hard to win at as the Boulevard. Arthur always said that he loved the cat calls and the threats shouted from the terraces, especially the 'Thre'penny stand'. There was a heavy atmospheric feeling at the Boulevard which greeted the players as they emerged from under the Best Stand to do battle. They knew just how hard it would be as they arrived at Airlie Street before the game. This occasion brought another 12–10 defeat for Leeds with Arthur racing over for two superb tries. York were beaten at Leeds 41–8, then came a close game down 't'lane' at Castleford where Leeds scampered to a 17–16 win on Good Friday.

Of the final seven games left in the season, six were at home so the Leeds faithful expected a flourish of good performances. From the Castleford game on 15th April, Leeds played matches: on 16th April against Featherstone Rovers at home (Leeds won 27–13); on 18th April against Castleford at home (Leeds won 30–4); on 19th April against Hull FC at home (Leeds won 46–11); on 22nd April against Bradford Northern at home (Leeds lost 7–2); on 25th April Leeds played Huddersfield away at Fartown (Leeds lost 36–0); and on 27th April faced Hull Kingston Rovers at home (Leeds won 22–10). Then in the final game of the season on 30th April Wakefield Trinity visited Headingley. They beat the home side 24–7. This was an incredible run of matches, eight games in 15 days. Of these eight games, Arthur played in four.

The season had taken its toll on the team with Bert Cook playing injured most of the time. At the end of the season Bert decided to make the trip back home to New Zealand to see if a complete rest and a bit of sunshine could help him recover fully from his niggling shoulder injury. This meant that he left the physical education teaching job at the City High School. It was an important section of the school's curriculum and the school had to find a good man to take over from Bert. Arthur Clues stepped in to fill the role. He took to teaching like a fish to water and also met his future wife Muriel Wood. She was the daughter of the owner of the City High School and treasurer of the Leeds Cricket, Football and Bowling Club. Arthur's forthright approach, his personality and his knowledge of fitness and how to make the fitness practices interesting made him a firm favourite with the pupils. Not long after returning to Leeds, Bert Cook started a tiling company in Leeds which he ran for a fair time.

Arthur played in 24 of Leeds' 44 games and scored seven tries. Two great servants of the Leeds club left during this season. Gareth Price played his final game for the club away at York on 29th January 1949 and scored Leeds' only try in the 9–7 win. He went on to captain Halifax at Wembley later that season. Dai Jenkins left after the final game of the season and joined Bramley. He had played in the only game to be played on the famous cricket field when Leeds beat Salford by 5–0 on Christmas Eve 1938.

The news had come through of the move to introduce another team into the tri nations tournament run each season between England, France and Wales. With enough Welshmen playing in the Rugby Football League to select a very strong team and the French coming good, it was decided to form a side composed of overseas players born outside the other three competing nations. With the number of top overseas players in the UK the team was certain to be an extremely strong one. Fixtures were drawn up to give this overseas team a build up before the actual four nation competition began. It was a very hard start indeed for the new team (called the Other Nationalities), as it was to take on England at Workington on 19th September 1949. At last there was a representative side for the overseas players to play for. This added an edge to an already intense weekly league programme. The number of new Aussie players regularly coming into the country meant it would be a hard team to break into.

Great Britain also had a tour due in 1950. There was an incentive for the local players to play well this coming term. As the season approached news came from Headingley that the exciting young centre-wingman, Tommy Wright, would again try a come back from his sickening knee problem. With the loss of Dai Jenkins the young local lad, Johnny Feather, was earmarked for an extended run at scrum half. It was also common knowledge that Leeds had long been an admirer of the clever and crafty Hunslet half back and utility player, Frank Watson.

5

ANOTHER REPRESENTATIVE ERA

Arthur missed the first three games of the 1949–1950 season but he went on to play in 27 games out of a possible 43 for Leeds. This was an age of brutal forward play. Few forwards tackled around the legs. Some forwards did tackle around the legs and were renowned for it, but the majority hit from the chest up. A head shot was the order of the day and only in extreme circumstances was the game stopped for a high tackle. The regular punishment from these hard body and head shots took its toll on most players. This was Arthur's fourth season at Headingley and the previous seasons he maintained a high ratio of games played. In his first season, starting on 1st February, he played in 19 games out of a possible 21. The following season it was 36 out of 46. Then in the 1948–1949 season he played 24 out of 44 games. His high pain threshold can be noted from these figures, although he did have injuries (plus a few suspensions along the way as was the norm in those days).

Arthur missed the first three games which were York away which Leeds won 25–15, Workington home which Leeds won 10–8 and Hull FC away, which Leeds lost 18–11. His return to action saw a win against York at Headingley 63–3 and Arthur scored two tries in a victory that saw him back to his best with rampaging bursts and try making runs. Hull Kingston Rovers travelled to Headingley next and Arthur crossed the line again in a 26–10 win. This game also saw the brave Tommy Wright, the talented Scottish try scorer, once again attempt a come-back. The following Wednesday 7th September, Leeds went to Central Park to take on the mighty Wigan who had started the season in great style. The teams were, Wigan: Martin Ryan; Gordon Ratcliffe, Jack Broome, Ernie Ashcroft, Brian Nordgren; Cec Mountford, Tommy Bradshaw; Ken Gee, Joe Egan, Frank Barton, Nat Silcock, Ted Slevin and Bill Hudson. Leeds: Bert Cook; Tommy Wright, Bob Bartlett, Ike Proctor, Ted Verrenkamp; Dickie Williams, Johnny Feather; Bob McMaster, Ken Kearney, Alan Kendrick, Arthur Clues, Denis Murphy and Des Clarkson. The gate of 25,000 spectators was roaring from the kick off as Wigan opened with some scintillating passing that had the big Kiwi wingman, Nordgren, racing for the corner flag only to be halted by a terrific Bob Bartlett tackle. Mountford was a constant threat as his speed off the mark and his strength of hand off caused problems for the Leeds middle backs. It was Cec Mountford who broke the deadlock when he seized onto a pass in midfield and sliced between Des Clarkson and Denis Murphy with an electric burst. He veered into Bert Cook then outside again to outpace the Leeds full back and dive in for a beautiful unconverted solo try. Cook landed a long range penalty goal to bring Leeds back into the game but the strong Nordgren, using his pace to hold off Feather and his strength to crash through Cook's gallant effort to tackle him, went over for another brilliant try to send Wigan in at half time leading 6–2. Within a minute of the second half opening, Mountford was heavily tackled by Clues and Clarkson and received a calf tear that left him a limping passenger on the wing. Leeds aimed attack after attack at the limping Kiwi but staunch Wigan covering halted each one. Gee kicked a penalty goal for Wigan to give them an 8–2 lead. Then as Ratcliffe lost the ball in a tackle,

Clarkson picked up and charged some 20 yards to score for Cook to convert and bring the score to 8–7 to Wigan. Attempting a clearing kick under extreme pressure, Mountford's kick was charged down by Kearney who picked up and fed Arthur a good 30 yards out. The big Aussie strode out and crossed the line easily outpacing the Wigan cover tacklers for Cook to convert. In front now by 12–8, Leeds looked to have this tough game in the bag but another penalty goal by Ken Gee took the score to 12–10. Arthur and Ken Gee were sent off as full time loomed for a toe-to-toe scrap, this was because the hardened warriors had old scores to settle. The injured Mountford looked like he could hardly move out on the wing as the final scrum of the game was set some 60 yards out from the Leeds line and as the referee called, 'One more tackle boys!' Bradshaw put the ball into the scrum tunnel. The scrum was set about 10 yards in from the touch line on which stood Mountford. As the ball came out of the pack to Bradshaw, Mountford, obviously kidding to the extent of his injury, came off the wing, in an arc, and took Bradshaw's pass in the stand off position. He sliced at full pace between Dickie Williams and Bob Bartlett and headed towards his close mate and fellow Kiwi, the dangerous Nordgren. Chased all the way by Dickie Williams, Mountford produced a classic dummy to Nordgren that had Ike Proctor, Ted Verrenkamp and Bert Cook flying across to save their line. All three bought the dummy to open up a clear run to the line, then as Mountford beat Williams' despairing last ditch attempt at a tackle, the crafty Kiwi hurled himself over for a brilliant last second try that gave the game to Wigan by 13–12. The post match newspaper report said that an ecstatic Wigan supporter told Mrs Mountford that Cec could have her husbands week's bacon ration as he was so exited about the try. The Mountford try went into Wigan folklore as one of the most exiting and uplifting tries ever seen at Central Park.

The Yorkshire Cup was next up and the draw pitted Leeds against the very strong Huddersfield side with the first leg at Fartown. Tommy Wright's try and Bert Cook's conversion gave Leeds their only points in the 13–5 defeat. The second leg was played two days later on Monday 12th September. The Leeds supporters saw another defeat, this time 16–8, with Arthur and Ted Verrenkamp scoring tries. The Headingley result gave the Fartowners an aggregate of 29–13.

Arthur then began a three match suspension for the Ken Gee dust up and he missed the Hunslet game at home. This was a devastating 12–2 defeat followed by another bad result at Hull Kingston Rovers (a 20–18 loss). In this game Wilf Cox stood in at full back for the injured Bert Cook and Cox landed three goals to go with Arthur Staniland's two tries and one each to Bob McMaster and Tommy Lane who was in the second row for the suspended Arthur. A little sunshine came back into the Leeds supporters' lives on 1st October when Leeds went across to Parkside and beat Hunslet 21–13 in a rousing game. Frank Watson made a big impression on his debut for Leeds against his old club.

On 19th September, the Other Nationalities had played their first game against England at Workington and had remarkably won through 13–7. The details were then published for the Other Nationalities second game against a tough Wales side at Abertillery. Arthur was selected to make his first appearance for the side but before this there was a little matter of two league games against Keighley. The first game was at Headingley and Leeds welcomed Arthur back as he led the forwards in great style and scored one of his specials, a side stepping thrust to the line from 25 yards out. This result was a 39–10 win for Leeds. The following week at Lawkholme Lane, Arthur scored two tries in a 22–5 win. Then the time came for Arthur's reappearance on the grand stage – he relished those big games.

Saturday 22nd October 1949 was the second game for the Other Nationalities side and Arthur was in the team to face Wales at the Rugby Union stronghold of Abertillery. Unfortunately the game attracted a meagre gate of just over 2,000 spectators. This constituted a financial loss on the day (as had the previous Wales v France game at Swansea). Most Welsh people at Abertillery had come to see how the former Rugby Union stars were performing and to see if they had picked up any bad league habits. The teams were very strong and the game was very competitive as the Welsh boys had pride at stake in their return to their homeland. They wanted to make a good show. Wales had out a big, experienced pack with plenty of pace in the backs. The line up was, Wales: Sid Williams [Salford]; Arthur Daniels [Halifax], Joe Mahoney [Dewsbury], Norman Harris [Leigh], Les Williams [Hunslet]; Jack Davies [Salford], Billy Banks [Huddersfield]; Tom Danter [Hull FC], Frank Osmond [Swinton], Eynon Hawkins [Salford], Trevor Foster [Bradford Northern], Derek Howes [Wakefield Trinity] and Bryn Goldswain [Oldham]. Other Nationalities: Johnny Hunter [Huddersfield]; Brian Bevan [Warrington], Tony Paskins [Workington Town], Pat Devery [Huddersfield], Lionel Cooper [Huddersfield]; Cec Mountford [Wigan], Duncan Jackson [Hull FC]; Bob McMaster [Leeds], Ken Kearney [Leeds], Harry Bath [Warrington], Arthur Clues [Leeds], Jim Payne [Hull FC] and Dave Valentine [Huddersfield]. The referee was Mr Charlie Appleton [Warrington].

Norman Harris the Welsh centre who joined Leigh from Oldham and later went to Rochdale Hornets, was a good footballer. He passed these skills onto his grandson, the excellent Iestyn Harris. The Welsh side put up a stern performance against this strong overseas outfit and although the weather was abysmal with heavy rain throughout the game, it helped keep the scores close. Against some of the league's best players, the home team pushed and harried their opponents all the way in the atrocious conditions before the visitors won 6–5. Two 'specials' by the two best wingmen in the world, Brian Bevan and Lionel Cooper, proved just too much for the brave home side. Bevan's try was a typical speedy effort with a blistering turn of pace along the touch line and a turn of foot on the slippery turf. This was too much for Williams, the Wales and Salford full back, as Bevan waltzed passed him. The Cooper try had all the hallmarks of that big, powerful wingman as he stormed over from close in using his pace and strength. The Welsh replied with a try and goal from the busy stand off, Jack Davies of Salford. Tradition says that both captains, Pat Devery and Trevor Foster, asked the referee if he would consider abandoning the game because of the horrible conditions but Charlie Appleton refused as this was considered an international game. So it was played to the bitter end with no one able to deal with the treacherous underfoot conditions other than Bevan and Cooper. Arthur, Harry Bath and Dave Valentine revelled in the muddy morass and all three had mighty games. This game was the first time since the New South Wales v Queensland game in Australia that Arthur joined Harry Bath in what became the finest partnership of two forwards ever seen in this country. Bath was selected for this game at blind side prop and to really show how versatile he was he represented the Other Nationalities at both hooker and in the second row but it was the Clues-Bath second row partnership that cemented their place in folklore.

Arthur resumed playing for Leeds on Bonfire Night. The game was played in the afternoon and there were plenty of fireworks at the old Barley Mow when both Bob Bartlett and

Denis Murphy returned to their former club to play for Leeds. Arthur supported his team mates in plenty of skirmishes. The team of local Bramley lads performed creditably but Leeds won 19–2.

Bradford Northern were visitors to Headingley. There was usually a battle when these traditional enemies clashed. The two who always seemed to have a go at each other were Arthur and Ken Traill and in this game it was just the same. The game was stopped on several occasions by the referee who read the riot act to both sets of forwards. A solid performance by Leeds gave them an 8–2 victory against a Northern side which contained all their top players.

This period proved to be a golden one for Arthur as he suddenly found his try scoring touch. Belle Vue Rangers, the grand old club that had evolved from the famous turn of the century team, Broughton Rangers, were the next opponents for Leeds. The Yorkshire club travelled to the Belle Vue complex in Manchester to take on the Rangers in their wide blue and white hooped jerseys. The complex at Belle Vue consisted of a huge funfair with all the exciting rides of the day, a zoo with a large array of animals and a stadium which housed not only the Belle Vue Rangers Rugby League Club but also the world famous Belle Vue speedway track which wound round the rugby field. The speedway team at Belle Vue were very successful with international stars riding for them. The team drew in big crowds to watch their home fixtures. The Rangers were a rough, tough side who beat most visitors on their tight playing area using a solid pack and excellent wingmen such as Stan McCormick. But Leeds were in a defiant mood and strode to a very good 15–10 win at Belle Vue with Dickie Williams, Ike Proctor and Arthur scoring tries and Bert Cook kicking three goals.

Halifax, another side who wore blue and white hoops came to Headingley next. Again Leeds showed tremendous resilience to win 17–7, Arthur again producing one of his specials to charge 30 yards for a cracking try. Proctor and Frank Watson scored a try each and Cook landed four goals. A shock was waiting for Leeds though on the first weekend in December in a visit to Crown Flatt, Dewsbury. Arthur was injured for this particular game, and the 14–2 defeat brought them back to earth. The week after, Arthur crossed twice for tries in the 40–2 win over Featherstone Rovers at Leeds. Bert Cook also scored two tries and Leeds changed goal kickers for this game, Des Clarkson kicking five conversions.

The hectic time of Christmas and the New Year was almost upon the clubs now and Leeds faced the traditional visit of Batley. They won the game 12–9 and a week later travelled to Mount Pleasant on Christmas Eve for the return fixture. Leeds won the game 27–16 and Arthur tore over for a try and led the pack in great style. On Boxing Day, Leeds faced another derby match when they hosted Wakefield Trinity and again Arthur romped over for a try in the 32–3 win. The day after, Bramley were beaten 30–10 at Headingley and on the last day of 1949, the mighty Wigan were beaten by 15–6 at Leeds. This game saw an unusual event in the Leeds club's history. A Rugby Union wingman from Ireland was given a one off trial game. This was unusual because those playing trial matches were almost always in the 'A' team. They would never be thrown in against the likes of Wigan. But play this young man did. His surname was O'Farrell and although he scored a popular try, cheered all the way as he ran in from around 40 yards out, he was seen only once again in the Leeds colours. This was at Halifax two days later where Leeds lost the game 20–0. Arthur, Bert Cook and Denis Murphy were missing from the side walloped at Thrum Hall. Tommy Lane played for Arthur, Wilf Cox for Bert Cook and Alan Kendrick for Denis Murphy.

With Arthur indisposed for three weeks Leeds, as they did

in those days, went out to Warrington and signed the well respected Welsh forward, Bill Hopper. Bill was a big man, standing 6 feet 4 inches tall and weighing well over 16 stone. He had decimated the Leeds defence in the previous season with a storming display. Leeds did not hesitate in signing this prop or second rower. Hopper's debut game was against Wakefield Trinity at Belle Vue and he helped in a 16–10 win.

The solid Belle Vue Rangers were beaten by 10–3 at Leeds on the 14th January 1950 by a strange looking Leeds team. It was: Cox; Staniland, T.L. Williams, Proctor, Turnbull; Dicky Williams, Feather; Prosser, Battersby, Kendrick, Hopper, Murphy and Clarkson.

The following day, Arthur, Bob Bartlett, Bob McMaster and Ken Kearney all played in the third game for the Other Nationalities in a match against France in Marseilles. In the early 1950s France were becoming a real force in international rugby league and in fact, went out to Australia and beat the Kangaroos on their own turf. The French were a side that played with superb flair but could also dish it out when called for. Marseilles at that time was something of a rugby league stronghold and an excellent crowd of over 20,000 turned out to cheer on their heroes. The Other Nationalities made one or two changes from the sodden game in Wales, notably the two main strike players, Brian Bevan and Lionel Cooper were both out injured, as was Arthur's side kick Harry Bath. But it was still a strong side that ran out in vastly different weather to last game. The South of France winter sunshine was much more comfortable than the Welsh torrential rain. Other Nationalities called on: Johnny Hunter [Huddersfield]; Bob Bartlett [Leeds], Tony Paskins [Workington Town], Pat Devery [Huddersfield], Brian Nordgren [Wigan]; Cec Mountford [Wigan], Duncan Jackson [Hull FC]; Bob McMaster [Leeds], Ken Kearney [Leeds], John Daley [Huddersfield], Arthur Clues [Leeds], Bob

Robson [Huddersfield] and Dave Valentine [Huddersfield]. The French were a greatly underestimated side and this team of January 1950 included many players who went on to lengthy international careers.. Led by the charismatic goal kicking full back, Robert Aubert-Puig, who decided to shorten that name to one that became famous throughout the rugby league playing world: Puig-Aubert. The team was: Puig-Aubert; V. Cantoni, G. Comes, P. Dejean, R. Contrastin; C. Galoup, R. Duffort; A. Ulma, G. Genoud, A. Beraud, H. Berthomieu, E. Brousse, and R. Pereze.

The Other Nationalities tactics were simple. Bob McMaster, John Daley and Arthur would upset any game plan of the French by late tackles, stiff arm tackles and any other devious tactic that they could. They also had to play their normal game when attacking. The referee, M. Guidecelli, had to take all sorts of barracking from the French team by way of protests at the high tackling, as they were knocked from pillar to post by Arthur and company. Retaliation had to come and it did in the huge shape of Ulma and Beraud the two French props. John Daley was knocked down but not out as Arthur and Wallaby Bob McMaster tore into the French who seemed to be mustering for an attack. Daley was back on his feet seeking revenge and the three big Other Nationalities forwards took on the whole of the French pack. Dave Valentine stood his ground and along with Bob Robson and Ken Kearney, watched the backs of the big three and acted as a rearguard as things ran out of steam. The French referee was out of his depth and had totally lost control of the proceedings. All credit to the French boys, they never lost control of their defence and tackled like demons to keep out Bob Bartlett, Pat Devery, Cec Mountford and Dave Valentine in quick succession before Bartlett raced in for an unconverted try after superb passing by Arthur, Valentine, Tony Paskins and Mountford. Immediately the French counter attacked as only the French can and scored a marvellous long range try after dazzling passing flashed through at least eight pairs of hands to give Contrastin a walk in by the posts, Dejean converting. Another brawl saw Brousse led from the field with blood gushing from a Clues right cross to the eye. There was still no word from the referee. Brousse returned, bandaged and whilst several of the forwards were seeking revenge, Contrastin raced away for a splendid second try. This effort ended the scoring and gave a hard earned win to France by 8–3.

Years later a newspaper article written by the brilliant French full back, Puig-Aubert, told of this game being the most brutal of all the matches he played in. Because the Other Nationalities forwards made a brawl of the game, their outstanding match winning backs were ignored. With the terrific Paskins and Devery outside the mercurial Cec Mountford and with two powerful and pacy wingman in Bartlett and Nordgren plus the magical running of Johnny Hunter, one would have thought that the biff, bang, wallop should have been saved for later. Another thing that Arthur used to say was that because of the injury to Harry Bath, the overseas team lacked another good footballer, as whilst the other forwards could have been battling, Bath would have been playing football and creating openings.

The summer of 1950 saw another tour of Australia and New Zealand. This meant that all the top players in the United Kingdom would be playing their hearts out to gain a place on the tour. Everyone wanted to catch the eye of the selectors. Arthur returned to Leeds in time for the long trip up to Workington Town. In another fighting match, he was sent off and given a three match suspension. The result at Workington ended with Leeds losing by a 13–2 margin.

The Challenge Cup campaign began with a first leg home

The Lions Tourists v New South Wales at the Sydney Cricket Ground.
Arthur, on the left, keeps his eye on the ball and Doug Phillips!

Arthur takes up the ball for Leeds against Wigan in the snow.

Arthur plays a physical game against arch opponent Ken Traill.

The Leeds team in 1950. Left to right, standing: Clarkson, Ryan, Bartlett, Hopper, Clues, McMaster. Seated: Kearney, Brown, Cook, Watson, Poole. Front: Turnbull, Verrenkamp.

Heartbreak in the 1950 Challenge Cup semi final as Warrington score to go through to Wembley.

Big Arthur scores against Hunslet with Jacky Evans trying to tackle.

The Leeds team before the 1951 Challenge Cup semi final.

Someone's in for it! Big Arthur playing for Other Nationalities.

Got'cha! Big Arthur tackles for Other Nationalities against England.

Big Arthur in his pomp.

Arthur being carried off at the Boulevard courtesy of Monsieur Poncinet.

A caricature of Arthur playing for Hunslet.

Hunslet 1955. Left to right, back row: Clues, Shaw, James, Smith, Gunney, Waite, Hatfield. Front: Talbott, Snowden, Williams, Evans, Burnell, Williamson.

Hunslet v Halifax. Big Arthur (extreme right) keeps his focus on the opposition.

Arthur (left) in his role as coach with the 1960 Australian World Cup squad.

Arthur enjoys a game of golf with Ken Traill (centre) in later years.

Leeds RLFC John Player winning reception. Left to right: Harvey Standeven (physio), Maurice Bamford (coach), Terry Web (loose forward), Arthur Clues, Alf Rutherford (former secretary).

tie against Leigh and a 14–7 victory for Leeds. Some people thought that a seven point lead might not be enough to take to Hilton Park in the second leg. However a sterling defensive stint and a Bert Cook penalty goal meant that although Leeds were beaten 7–2 in this leg, the team had scored enough to go through on a 16–14 aggregate. Dewsbury were beaten at Headingley 17–3 in the league game and Arthur returned the following week to play Wigan at home in the second round of the Challenge Cup. Leeds were as strong as they could be with Bill Hopper making way for Arthur in the second row. The Team was: Cook; Staniland, Bartlett, Proctor, Verrenkamp; Dickie Williams, Watson; McMaster, Kearney, Prosser, Clues, Murphy and Clarkson. In a tough cup tie played before an all ticket full house of 37,144, a Dickie Williams try and two Bert Cook goals gave Leeds a passage through into round three by 7–2. Arthur scored again in the next game up at Craven Park, Barrow as Leeds lost by 14–8. Then, with the scent of Wembley in their nostrils, Leeds faced Wakefield Trinity at Headingley in round three.

The lead up to the quarter final was strange indeed. Trinity should have played local rivals Dewsbury in round two but because of frost, the match was postponed until Monday of round three week. The game ended in a 2–2 draw with the replay at Crown Flatt the following Wednesday. Three days before the Leeds cup tie two regular Trinity forwards, Jim Higgins and Harry Murphy, were sent off and Derek Howes, injured from the Belle Vue game, was not fit. The three games in five days had also caused injury to three more of the regular forwards so it was a very depleted pack that took the field for Trinity on 11th March. Another all ticket game proved beneficial for Leeds as in this third round tie the gate was another ground-filler with 37,114, just 30 people short of the Wigan gate in round two. The teams lined up with Leeds fielding the same side as in the Wigan game. Wakefield were:

Ernest Luckman; Dennis Baddeley, Don Froggett, Leighton Davies, Dennis Booker; Arthur Fletcher, Herbert Goodfellow; Jack Booth, Len Marson, Dennis Nutting, Des Foreman, Don Robinson and Reg Hughes. The pack that Wakefield were forced to play because of suspensions and injuries contained four men who had played for or would play for Leeds. Jack Booth and Des Foreman had played for Leeds and Dennis Nutting and Don Robinson would join the Headingley setup in the future.

This was an intriguing cup tie with the underdogs, Trinity, playing the leading role. Leeds started brightly with Bob Bartlett sent striding for the line by a great burst, a run and beautifully timed pass by Arthur. Unfortunately the Aussie centre fell to a last ditch Luckman tackle. Dickie Williams was held short and Des Clarkson too was almost over but for brilliant defence by the 17 year old Robinson and the much older Des Foreman. It was Foreman who gave Trinity the lead when he hit a perfect 55 yard penalty goal after being narrowly wide with a 60 yard effort earlier. Des Foreman was a prodigious kicker of a ball when all conditions were right and this mammoth kick cleared the crossbar with ease. Bert Cook replied immediately with a great penalty goal from 50 yards out to draw level but the clever Goodfellow opened Leeds up at will with his vast experience and his hidden strength of hand-off which he used to great effect. The crafty half back, using the dummy to send the Leeds defence the wrong way, produced a superb pass that had Arthur Fletcher darting to the line only to be stopped dead in his tracks by another Arthur (Clues) whose hard tackling and tough cup tie defence was frustrating the Wakefield pack. Then when Clues halted Leighton Davies near the line, Reg Hughes and Jack Booth took offence at his ferocity and set about Arthur in rare style. They did this without realising his resilience. Arthur flattened Hughes and was on top of Booth when the strong minded referee, Mr George Phillips of Widnes, ended the fisticuffs and awarded a penalty to Trinity. From the kick to touch, Goodfellow's experience showed again as he grubber kicked between Clarkson and McMaster. As Clarkson hesitated a split second, Reg Hughes swooped on to the kick, picked up brilliantly and dived over for a well taken try. At 5–2 to Wakefield it was only justice as Trinity's depleted side had played wonderfully and only the non stop efforts of Arthur Clues had managed to keep trinity from adding to their lead. Just before half time, Leeds were awarded a penalty and Cook landed an impossible goal with a kick that was going wide but veered back between the posts in the final 10 yards of flight. It was an awesome kick that seemed to demoralise the brave Trinity side and sent the teams in with Wakefield holding just a one point advantage.

Wakefield exerted great pressure at the restart and after a lengthy spell of nail biting by the Leeds supporters, it was the Trinity faithful who drew breath at the sight of the big Australian forward, Clues, side stepping clear in a wonderful clearing run from almost on his own try line to be tackled by the gallant Ernest Luckman on the half way line. Then it was Wakefield's turn as the nippy Leighton Davies was sent clear by the barnstorming young Robinson. Davies rounded Cook with extra pace and looked all on a scorer until the alert Verrenkamp raced back and, with a beautifully timed leg tackle, saved the day for his team. Then the teenage Don Robinson went careering down the touch line like a runaway train, bursting through four tackles before hitting the unmovable figure of big Arthur, who wrestled the youngster into touch at the corner flag. With only a quarter of an hour to go and Leeds still behind by a point, Clarkson found a superb touch kick in his locker and this took play inside the Trinity 25. Leeds won the scrum and half back Frank Watson, who had played for several seasons for Hunslet alongside Des

Clarkson, used the old reverse pass routine with his former Parkside partner. Clarkson was held up on the Trinity line. A quick play the ball, five men handled and the final pass sent Bartlett slicing over in the far corner to run around in the in-goal to a position from which Cook converted. Ahead now for the first time in the game, Leeds relaxed to play some great football and only heroic Wakefield tackling kept them at bay. An attack by the Leeds backs was stopped about 30 yards from the Trinity line but from the play the ball a devastating burst, including two of the famous side steps by Arthur, ended with the big forward being tackled again by Luckman only yards from the line and as he was falling he turned to find that master footballer Frank Watson supporting at his shoulder. He made a neat pass and Watson was tearing under the posts for a grand try converted by Cook. The brave Trinity came back and in the final seconds, Len Marson sold a cheeky dummy to dive over for an unconverted try. Leeds were home and dry 14–8 and into the semi-final. Could this be the season that Arthur had dreamed of since the disappointing Wembley outing of 1947?

Leeds' opponents in the semi-final would be the tough Warrington outfit which had in its ranks Arthur's side kick in the Other Nationalities team, Harry Bath. This game was in three weeks' time. First there was a little matter of two league games, Bradford Northern at Odsal and Hull FC at home. The trip to Odsal brought about a good 15–5 win with Arthur again scoring one of his special tries, beating four tacklers in a 20 yard dash. Hull FC at Headingley saw a bright Leeds performance and another 19–4 win. On then to the biggest game of the season, Warrington at Odsal in the Challenge Cup semi-final.

Leeds made one change from the successful side that beat Wakefield Trinity. Bob McMaster was out injured so Dai

Prosser moved across to open side prop and Bill Hopper came in at blind side prop. The Warrington team was: Les Jones; Brian Bevan, Ron Ryder, Albert Naughton, Albert Johnson; Bryn Knowelden, Gerry Helme; Bill Darbyshire, Ike Fishwick, Jimmy Featherstone, Harry Bath, Bob Ryan, Harold Palin. Played before a huge crowd of almost 70,000, Leeds had hardly arrived on the pitch before the big Warrington prop Darbyshire had barged his way over near the corner flag. Warrington, in their jerseys of primrose and blue hoops, never gave Leeds the chance to settle and playing towards the Rooley Lane end it wasn't long before Harry Bath rubbed it in with a strong try. Finding a gap in the Leeds defensive line he aimed straight at Frank Watson and charged right over the top of him to plant the ball down. Still not finished, Albert Johnson scored the cheekiest of tries as he was put clear up the touch line. When approached by Bert Cook, Johnson sold the perfect dummy to Cook who bought it hook, line and sinker as Johnson pretended to pass inside then scooted into the corner for a great showman's try. As Bert Cook turned inside to challenge the Warrington support player he found that no one was there, Johnson had dummied to no one! Going in at half time Leeds had it all to do at 14–0 down. Although they tightened up considerably, Leeds could only muster two goals by Bert Cook. Winning the second half 4–2, Leeds had too much to do and the Wire marched on to Wembley by a winning margin of 16–4. Late in the game Des Clarkson was sent off mainly because of the frustration felt by all the Leeds players. Arthur felt the pain of this crushing psychological defeat more than most as he desperately wanted to return to Wembley to show what he could do on that vast stage.

The sad season ended with Leeds winning only two of the final six games. Castleford were beaten 12–10 at Headingley, Featherstone Rovers beat Leeds at Post Office Road 16–2,

Castleford won the return game at Wheldon Road 7–2, Huddersfield beat Leeds at Fartown 23–15 and two days later Huddersfield won at Headingley 22–8. Then in the final league game of the season, Halifax were beaten at Headingley 10–7. Arthur missed the two Huddersfield games serving a two match ban for being sent off at Featherstone but returned for the Halifax game when he had an excellent match playing at loose forward. This season also saw the end of brave Tommy Wright's come back attempts with his final game at Fartown in the last but one game of the season. T.L. [Les] Williams also retired at the end of the season as did the grand old war horse Dai Prosser, who ran his fish and chip business in York but returned to Leeds as coach. Arthur had a successful season scoring 16 tries in the 27 games he played. Another plus for the club was the debut on the last day of the season against Halifax of a young three-quarter from the local Burley Rugby Union club, Gordon Brown, who would soon make his mark as a regular first team player.

6

MORE SIGNINGS BUT NO CUPS

The big news in the close season was the signing of the strong running Australian wingman, Bruce Ryan from Hull FC. Bruce was a handsome man with film star good looks and he could play a bit too. He was also a nightclub singer and had the girls swooning. Bruce was a talented lad who played for Newtown just as Arthur made the Australian test side. The two men knew each other well. He had been a very popular player at the Boulevard and the Hull FC fans had taken the loss of such a good and well-liked player badly. Bruce Ryan was very powerfully built with a fair turn of speed and was just the tonic the Leeds crowd needed. The supporters of the Headingley club had been brought up watching good, exciting Australian wingmen for years.

Leeds also went to the Boulevard to sign the highly rated, hard tackling second row forward Bernard Poole, who wore a trademark black scrum cap. Bernard was brought up in the Morley area, just south of Leeds and formed a very effective partnership with Arthur which lasted four years. The partnership made its debut in the third game of the season at the Barley Mow ground, Bramley.

Dickie Williams was missing for the first few weeks of the new season as he had made the selection for the 1950 tour and would not be available until the end of September.

The opening game of the 1950–1951 season was at Headingley against a very strong Workington Town. The Leeds supporters needed a tonic win after the depressing end to the previous campaign. Town had developed into a fine footballing unit under the expert guidance of player-coach, Gus Risman (the former Great Britain captain against Arthur's 1946 Australian test side). The Workington team bristled with great players, Risman at full back, Tony Paskins and Eppie Gibson in the centre, Johnny Lawrenson and George 'Happy' Wilson, the 'Flying Scotsman' on the wings, Albert Pepperall at stand off and Jacky Thomas at scrum half. The pack was a typical Cumbrian big set with Jimmy Hayton, Vince McKeating and Jimmy 'Pongo' Wareing in the front row. The two Australians, Bevan Wilson (ex Wallaby international) and John Mudge played in the second row, and the great man of Cumbrian Rugby League, Billy Ivison played at loose forward. Leeds turned out a team which included seven overseas players. The team was: Wilf Cox; Drew Turnbull, Ike Proctor, Bob Bartlett, Bruce Ryan; Ted Verrenkamp, Frank Watson; Bob McMaster, Ken Kearney, Alan Kendrick, Des Clarkson, Denis Murphy and Arthur Clues. Leeds pleased their supporters no end as they won convincingly 29–15. Turnbull scored four tries and Ryan, Bartlett and Arthur crossed for one try each. Clarkson scored three tries with Cox adding goals.

The following Wednesday evening Leeds came a cropper when Keighley turned up the heat at Lawkholme Lane to win 9–7. Gordon Brown in the centre for the injured Bartlett and Bill Hopper in the second row for Murphy were the two Leeds changes. But Leeds got back to winning ways when they beat Bramley at the Barley Mow 25–10 in the game that saw Bernard Poole make a try scoring debut in the second row. Clarkson dropped back to number 13 for Arthur who had sprained an ankle and Maurice Ogden took Clarkson's second row spot. Cox and Kendrick added a try apiece to Poole's one. Clarkson kicked seven goals and Frank Watson made one drop goal.

Halifax were next up at Headingley and Leeds beat them

19–0. Bert Cook was back for Cox at full back, Frank Watson, such a versatile player, was in the centre for Proctor, Arthur Staniland was on the wing for Ryan, Feather was at number seven for Watson, Battersby hooked in place of Kearney, Clarkson was in for Ogden and Arthur was back at number 13 for Clarkson in a much changed Leeds side. Turnbull, in top form, scored two tries and Staniland one, with Cook landing five goals. Arthur was back in form and was the best Leeds forward on view.

The Yorkshire Cup rolled round again and Leeds took on the tough cup fighters, Featherstone Rovers at Post Office Road in the first leg and took back to Headingley a handy 20–7 lead, with Drew Turnbull racing over for another three tries to bring his total to nine tries in five games. Two days later Featherstone were beaten again 20–9 in the second leg at Leeds to put Leeds through on a 40–16 aggregate. Back in the league, Leeds beat Salford at the Willows 20–9. Arthur scored again to underline his good form and Poole, Verrenkamp, Bartlett, Hopper and Turnbull crossed for tries, with Clarkson landing one goal.

After loosing only one game in the first seven, Leeds lost to Wigan at home 23–12. Arthur was out injured and missed the big defeat by Huddersfield in the County Cup second round at Headingley when the Fartowners won 29–2. Still without Arthur, Leeds went to the Boulevard and the Hull FC supporters in the 'Thre'penny' stand voiced their opinion of the Hull directors as Leeds won 21–15 with Hull old boys scoring (Bruce Ryan scored two tries and Bernard Poole scored one). Other try scorers for Leeds were Gordon Brown and Frank Watson with Bert Cook adding three goals. Leeds beat Batley at Mount Pleasant 16–11 as the month changed from September to October.

On 4th October Arthur was selected for 'The Rest' to play the recently returned 1950 Great Britain Tourists at Wigan's Central Park. The Tourists team was: Martin Ryan [Wigan];

Arthur Daniels [Halifax], Ernest Ward [Bradford Northern], Ernie Ashcroft [Wigan], Tom Danby [Salford]; Jacky Cunliffe [Wigan], Tommy Bradshaw [Wigan]; Ken Gee [Wigan], Joe Egan [Leigh], Elwyn Gwyther [Belle Vue Rangers], Bob Ryan [Warrington], Fred Higgins [Widnes], Harry Street [Dewsbury]. This was a good side with a hard pack of forwards and fast backs. The Rest side was a mixture of various nationalities: Bert Cook [Leeds and New Zealand]; Brian Bevan [Warrington and Australia], Jack Broome [Wigan and England], Les Williams [Hunslet and Wales], Lionel Cooper [Huddersfield and Australia]; Cec Mountford [Wigan and New Zealand], Gerry Helme [Warrington and England]; Bob McMaster [Leeds and Australia], Len Marson [Wakefield Trinity and England], Alan Prescott [St Helens and England], Arthur Clues [Leeds and Australia], Ted Slevin [Wigan and England] and Dave Valentine [Huddersfield and Great Britain]. The referee was Mr Ron Gelder [Wakefield] and the attendance was 25,000. The captain of The Rest was Cec Mountford and the Tourists were good value to watch as they played some great rugby. Although the game held no great bite, the takings contributed to The Lord Derby Memorial Fund by almost £2,000. Harry Street opened the scoring with a neat try but The Rest took the lead when Jack Broome supported a Clues break to score a good try to which Cook added the conversion. Ernest Ward kicked a great penalty goal then combined with Jacky Cunliffe to score a try after Jacky had made the opening. Brian Bevan scored one of his specials and Cook goaled from the touch line. Ernest Ward equalised with another good penalty at 10 points all. Martin Ryan took control of the second half with a superb long range try in which he beat four would be tacklers. Then in quick succession he made two tries for Tom Danby and Ernest Ward kicked two goals. The crowd were delighted to witness another two cracking tries by Bevan and Lionel Cooper to give a score of 16–23 to the Great Britain Tourists.

Arthur had his usual go at Joe Egan and Ken Gee during the game and the crowd loved it, cheering Arthur's every move.

Arthur was rested for the Hull Kingston Rovers game at home, which Leeds won by 37–8 but Drew Turnbull, in a superb run of form, raced in for two further tries to again rattle the cages of the selectors. The tough test of Workington Town away came next as Arthur returned to lead the Leeds pack in great style and score a memorable long distance try in a fine win for Leeds of 14–13. Turnbull again showed rare pace in a 60 yard try scoring dash. Leeds beat Dewsbury at Headingley 27–6, showing that while the Crown Flatt side were an excellent home team, they were vulnerable when playing away. Turnbull with another two tries and Ryan, Proctor and Bill Hooper with one try each were beginning to show terrific form. Cook landed six goals. Arthur also had hit top form both for Leeds and Other Nationalities for whom his combination with Harry Bath was developing into a tremendous partnership. This seemed to spark a glut of rumours that Arthur was bound for Warrington to link up with Bath at club level. Then the rumours changed overnight with Bath joining Leeds to give the Yorkshire club their best ever forward combination. Neither moves ever happened of course, but the mind boggles at the thought of those two magnificent Aussies playing together regularly in club football.

Hunslet were well beaten at Parkside by 23–15 as Leeds then went 28 days without game. On the resumption of play, Leeds had a great surprise for their supporters with a fantastic win against the almost unbeatable Huddersfield at their Fartown home ground. Having easily beaten Leeds in the second round of the Yorkshire Cup at Headingley a defeat was on the cards but Arthur had one of his best ever games in the blue and amber jersey as Leeds went to a 17–16 victory. Bartlett, Ryan and Cook scored tries and Cook kicked four goals. Leeds then achieved a notable double over arch enemy

Hunslet with an 18–7 win at Headingley. Arthur continued his great form by scoring one of his special tries with a side step, a burst clear, chip over the full back, re-gather and sprint home. It was a wonderful effort. Ryan, Bartlett and Frank Watson, scoring again against his old club, added further tries and Cook claimed three goals. The dreaded visit to Crown Flatt brought the usual tough game and this time Leeds took a good hiding losing 28–6.

Arthur, Bert Cook, Bob Bartlett and Bob McMaster all missed the home defeat by 6–5 at the hands of Warrington on 9th December as they were selected for the Other Nationalities to play in Bordeaux against France on 10th December. This game in France was the prelude to a vicious vendetta between two players. Captained by the excellent Cec Mountford, the Other Nationalities fielded a very strong side with the versatile Harry Bath hooking in place of the injured Ken Kearney. The side was: Bert Cook [Leeds]; Brian Bevan [Warrington], Bob Bartlet [Leeds], Ian Clark [Huddersfield], Lionel Cooper [Huddersfield]; Cec Mountford [Wigan], Duncan Jackson [Hull FC]; Bob McMaster [Leeds], Harry Bath [Warrington], John Daly [Huddersfield], Arthur Clues [Leeds], John Mudge [Workington Town] and Dave Valentine [Huddersfield]. The French side was arguably, the best team the country ever produced as the following season they embarked on a full test tour of Australia and beat the Aussies on their own grounds. They were a terrific team and were captained by that wonderful player, Puig-Aubert from full back. The full French side was: Puig-Aubert; V. Cantoni, J. Crespo, Y. Treilhes, R. Contrastin; C. Galoup, R. Duffort; L. Mazon, M. Martin, A. Bernaud, E. Ponsinet, E. Brousse and G. Calixte. The referee was M. Vacher, a local man and the attendance was just over 28,000.

With typical French panache, the home team had the visitors running every which-way. Impossible passes were thrown and taken by the French in that superb way they played back then. With tremendous support play and gilt edged entertainment, they had the Other Nationalities on the back foot from the kick off. The strong French pack also bossed the set scrums and this made the visitor's task even harder. With little or no ball, the defensive stint proved too much for the overseas outfit and after Puig-Aubert had landed a superb penalty goal, a fantastic passing move, started on their own 25 line, saw eight players handle with exquisite skill before Galoupe found Crespo with a great wide pass and the quick centre sped over the line on around 25 minutes, Puig-Aubert converting with another fine kick. The crowd were ecstatic at the quality of the French play but in that first half they saw a cloud appear as the big Edouard Ponsinet, the French second row forward and Marseille policeman, clashed momentarily with ex policeman, Arthur Clues, in midfield. A couple of punches were exchanged but that was the end of it, or so everyone thought.

Within minutes of the second half kick off, Other Nationalities were back in the game. A thrust by Arthur, support by Dave Valentine and the ball was in the hands of Cec Mountford who sized up the situation in a second and flung a long pass out to the maestro on the wing, Brian Bevan, who set off to outpace all the French cover in a 60 yard run. France took play back to the visitors' 25 area and a crashing run from the strong L. Mazon, saw the big French prop show both pace and evasive qualities to register a fine try which Puig-Aubert converted. The French full back star kicked another two goals to complete the scoring and produce a good result for the French with a score of 16–3 to France. Late in the game, after a series of hits by Ponsinet and Clues on each other, the big Frenchman was clearing his line with a powerful run when Arthur went in at him with a hard, high tackle. The thud was heard by everyone in the ground as the Frenchman went down as if pole axed. One problem was that just as Arthur arrived with the high tackle, Ponsinet ducked to avoid it but only managed to duck into it. The result was a very serious head injury to the Frenchman. Many of the players were shocked at the sight of the injury inflicted as in Arthur's own words, 'It looked as if I had scalped him and that his hairline was a few inches higher than normal.' Ponsinet's head was gashed wide open and it was obvious that the duck into the swinging arm had caused a massive amount of damage. Ponsinet was carried off and that was that. France won well on the day and their form was to continue on the superb tour the following year.

Leeds had another two weeks off after the home defeat by Warrington and play resumed at Headingley with a 23rd December game against Featherstone Rovers, which Leeds won 15–13. Christmas Day saw Batley beaten 21–2 and Arthur added another good try to his mounting total this season. The next game for Leeds was at Headingley again on 6th January 1951 when the big Hull FC pack arrived to do battle. Another Leeds win started the New Year in good style as the tough Hull FC were beaten 33–2. Drew Turnbull claimed another four tries in his second quartet of the season. Arthur maintained his scoring average when he romped over twice in the big 46–12 victory over the old enemy, Wakefield Trinity at Leeds and Turnbull scored another two tries in this the fifth straight home game for Leeds. An away match to Wigan at Central Park was the next hurdle for Leeds and awaiting them there was a 21–13 defeat. This was only their fifth league defeat in 21 games.

The Challenge Cup was just around the corner and there was a confident feeling at the club that they could do well this time. Arthur still yearned for another Wembley appearance as the Leeds side awaited news of their first round opponents. It was the hard to beat Oldham, with the first vital leg at home. Leeds beat Salford in the league 17–14 with Alan Horsfall scoring the only try for Leeds. The side scored seven goals, six by Cook and one by Clarkson. In the Challenge Cup a comprehensive 23–5 win at Headingley offered some breathing space for the second leg at the Watersheddings the following Saturday. Oldham won this leg 13–10 and therefore Leeds went through on a 36–15 aggregate. The second round draw gave 'lucky' Leeds another home tie against the very dangerous Leigh but they first had a trip to Wilderspool to meet Warrington. The 'Wire' proved too strong again for Leeds who lost 24–16.

Leigh came to Leeds in the cup on 3rd March and a wonderful hat trick of tries by Bruce Ryan together with a Dickie Williams special, added to four Bert Cook goals gave Leeds a solid 20–3 win. A good result against Huddersfield at Headingley would put the squad in a great frame of mind for the third round tie, again at Headingley, against Halifax. Leeds beat Huddersfield 18–5 with Bruce Ryan scoring two further tries. Everything now depended on this vital third round, the round which almost every professional player admits is the crucial one. Halifax had a tough pack and Arthur knew this was the problem. Leeds had to overcome the big, tough Halifax pack. With their strongest team available, Leeds had to follow a simple game plan to travel into the semi-final. The forwards had to take the Halifax pack head on and create enough space for Dickie Williams and Frank Watson to get the ball to the prolific scorers Drew Turnbull and Bruce Ryan. In a ding dong struggle, the Leeds pack of McMaster, Kearney, Hopper, Clues, Poole and Clarkson worked the game plan superbly. Bartlett and Turnbull scored two of the three Leeds tries. The third try was scored by the forward of the game, Arthur Clues. His try broke the Halifax spirit as he used guile, strength and pace to straighten onto a Dickie Williams pass and thunder over for his best try of the season. Cook added three goals in this 15–7 great cup win in which every player played his part.

111

With just over a month to the semi-final there were several big games to play before the last step to Wembley, including an international match, Other Nationalities v Wales at St Helens, Swansea, on 31st March.

Keighley were the visitors to Headingley and left defeated by 25–10, next were Castleford and they too fell to the pace of the Leeds backs as the Loiners won a 27–4 victory. In these two matches, Ryan scored three tries and Turnbull scored two. Arthur missed the Featherstone Rovers away game but Leeds, with Denis Murphy filling yet another position this time as centre to Drew Turnbull, pulled off another well earned victory with Turnbull benefiting from Murphy's service with another two tries.

Arthur was back with a bang for the trip to Castleford and scored a cracking try in the 22–5 win. In fact all the back three crossed the line in this game, Poole and Clarkson notching up a try apiece to go with yet another try from the Flying Scotsman, Drew Turnbull, plus five goals from Cook. Bramley made Leeds fight all the way in a tight derby match at Headingley. Turnbull and Cook crossed the line for tries and Cook landed four goals in a very close 14–6 win.

On 31st March, the St Helens ground in Swansea hosted the second Wales v Other Nationalities game. Again the attendance was poor with a gate of just 5,000. It was a poor crowd because the Rugby Football League had sponsored an eight team Welsh League in an effort to stoke up interest in the principality. One solitary player from this league gained selection in a very strong side, blind side prop forward, Mel Ford [Aberavon] but even this would not tempt the locals into attending the game in droves. The two sides had been selected with a win in mind, Wales: Jack Evans [Hunslet]; Roy Lambert [Dewsbury], Don Gullick [St Helens], Les Williams [Hunslet], Terry Cook [Halifax]; Dickie Williams [Leeds], Billy Banks [Huddersfield]; Dai Harris [Castleford],

Frank Osmond [Swinton], M. Ford [Aberavon], George Parsons [St Helens], Ray Cale [St Helens] and Glanville James [Hunslet]. Other Nationalities selected a tough side but had the two famous wingmen, Bevan and Cooper, plus the former Australian Rugby Union centre and captain, Trevor Allan complete with scrum cap alongside another fine Australian, Tony Paskins. The full team was: Bert Cook [Leeds]; Brian Bevan [Warrington], Trevor Allan [Leigh], Tony Paskins [Workington Town], Lionel Cooper [Huddersfield]; Peter Henderson [Huddersfield], Ike Proctor [Leeds]; John Mudge [Workington Town], Ken Kearney [Leeds], John Daly [Huddersfield], Arthur Clues [Leeds], Bob Robson [Huddersfield] and Dave Valentine [Huddersfield]. The referee was Mr Albert Dobson [Pontefract].

There was much interest in the Welsh newspapers about the overseas team stand off half, Peter Henderson. Peter had represented New Zealand as a 100 metres sprinter in the Olympic Games and my word, he was quick. Peter played a lot of his Rugby League for Huddersfield as a free scoring wing three-quarter but his pace at stand off was devastating. Other Nationalities had the unusual statistics of all their back division being scorers. Bert Cook kicked three goals and all remaining backs scored tries. Henderson's touchdown brought the house down as he showed off his breathtaking speed in a 60 yard run. Bevan and Cooper each produced a masterpiece of their own when Bevan mesmerised the Welsh defence with a mazy run of 50 yards and Cooper blasted over from 30 yards but demolished three defenders on his way to score. The classy Allan and Paskins each ran with silky smoothness for their tries and Proctor's effort exhibited the famous Maori sidestep when he ploughed straight through two defenders who thought they had been hit by a cyclone. The other try was scored by the one and only big Arthur who side stepped, dummied and swerved past four tacklers on his way to the line. For Wales, who played their part in a most entertaining game, although losing 27–21, Terry Cook scored two super tries, Don Gullick used his strength to power over, Glanville James scored a neat touchdown and M. Ford ran well for a big man to register his debut try. Jacky Evans kicked three good goals as the open game came to an end, the only disappointment being the attendance.

Arthur missed the 22–14 defeat for Leeds at Knowsley Road against the Saints but the week after became another cup nightmare for the Leeds supporters. Leeds' opponents in the semi-final were the tough cup fighters from Barrow and the game was to be played at Odsal on Saturday 7th April. The Shipbuilders had always given Leeds a hard time in cup ties and this epic game, full of excitement right to the final whistle, was certainly a hard game. Leeds came into this semi-final as clear favourites. The other semi-final, Wigan v Warrington at Swinton, allowed the traditional Leeds supporters to hope for a final long waited for, a Leeds v Wigan showpiece at Wembley. But first, Leeds had to remove Barrow from the equation. The teams were, Leeds: Cook; Turnbull, Feather, Proctor, Ryan; Dickie Williams, Watson; Horsfall, Kearney, Hopper, Clues, Poole and Clarkson. Looking now at that Barrow side one must accept that it was a very good team but at the time it seemed a little old and slow, it was however, excellent on the day. The Barrow, team were: Stretch; Lewthwaite, Jackson, Goodwin, Castle; Willie Horne, Toohey; Longman, McKinnell, Hartley, Grundy, Atkinson and McGregor. Barrow's backs alone should have indicated their great potential. The best pair of club wingmen, Jim Lewthwaite and Frank Castle, the centres Phil Jackson and Dennis Goodwin who went on in to legend, the most innovative rugby league player of his era, Willie Horne and his box of tricks partner at scrum half, the Great Britain international, Ted Toohey. Of the Barrow team that played Leeds in the snow of 1947, only Jim Lewthwaite, Willie

Horne and tough prop, Frank Longman remained. Leeds too had only three players on duty that appeared in that morass of snow and mud at Headingley four years earlier, Bert Cook, Dickie Williams and big Arthur. Bob McMaster pulled out of the original team with an injury and utility forward, the reliable Alan Horsfall, came in. Defences were tough as one would expect from a semi-final and this suited Arthur who was again the most penetrative Leeds forward. But, metaphorically speaking, this game has a funny way of sometimes kicking players in the teeth, and going into the final minutes of this hard fought game with master goal kicker Willie Horne unable to take any kicks because of a leg injury, Barrow were awarded a penalty kick some 30 yards out right on the touch line side. The giver of this 'safe' penalty kick was Arthur Clues, who took revenge on an earlier hit on him but his retaliation was seen by the referee. Leeds were in front by 14–12 and normal time was over. This would be the final act of a particularly hard game. With Horne unavailable to kick, the Barrow captain called up the tall, slim full back, Harry Stretch. Stretch had just made the team owing to the retirement of the great Joe 'Cowboy' Jones. Stretch was not the regular goal kicker but up he came, cool as a cucumber, placed the ball down and kicked a wonder goal from that touch line shot. I can see him now, being submerged by his team mates as the referee ended the game at 14 apiece.

Wigan had beaten Warrington by 3–2 at Swinton so Leeds and Barrow had to replay at Fartown the following Wednesday. Almost 60,000 spectators had attended Odsal on the Saturday and for the replay around 33,000 crammed into Fartown on Wednesday 11th April. It was a fairy tale outing for Barrow, completely outplaying a Leeds side that had several changes. Proctor moved into the right centre for Johnny Feather, Gordon Brown took Proctor's berth, Bruce Ryan went out for Arthur Staniland to move onto the left wing and Alan Horsfall lost his place to Maurice Ogden. A crushing

28–13 win was recorded to the valiant Barrow fighters who went on to Wembley only to loose to Wigan 10–0.

This was another blow to Arthur but the big Aussie had given away the penalty that cost Leeds a much coveted Wembley appearance.

As often happened at Leeds, once out of the Challenge Cup, the season was virtually over and of the final six league games left, Leeds won only one. The sequence went: Saints, away, lost 9–3; Bradford Northern at home, lost 17–8 (Arthur scored a good try); Wakefield Trinity away, lost 26–18; Hull Kingston Rovers home, won 26–20; Halifax away, lost 17–11; and finally, Bradford Northern away, lost 15–14.

In the 1950–1951 season Arthur played in 31 of the 45 games scheduled for Leeds and scored 12 tries. Bernard Poole was the only forward to play more club games than Arthur when he recorded 39 games played out of the 45.

The international season did not finish when the league closed down for the summer. The Festival of Britain began in May 1951. This was a festival to commemorate the Second World War victory and Britain's march forward in issues such as medicine, world trade and peace. Arthur was invited to play in a classic fixture, Great Britain v Australasia at Headingley on 19th May 1951 as rugby league's tribute to the festival. With Mr Charlie Appleton as referee, the game was attended by a very healthy 16,000 spectators. It was of course an honour to be selected and two strong sides lined up before the kick off to be presented to various dignitaries. The Great Britain side was: Jacky Evans [Hunslet]; Jack Hilton [Wigan], Ernest Ward [Bradford Northern], Jack Broome [Wigan], Terry Cook [Halifax]; Eric Hesketh [Saints], Russell Pepperell [Huddersfield]; Ken Gee [Wigan], Frank Osmond [Swinton], Jack Booth [Wakefield Trinity], Nat Silcock [Wigan], George Parsons [Saints] and Dave Valentine [Huddersfield]. Australasia fielded a top side with all the crowd pleasing players in place; it was: Joe Phillips [Bradford Northern]; Brian Bevan [Warrington], Trevor Allen [Leigh], Pat Devery [Huddersfield], Lionel Cooper [Huddersfield]; Peter Henderson [Huddersfield], Ike Proctor [Leeds]; Jim Payne [Hull FC], Ken Kearney [Leeds], John Mudge [Workington Town], Arthur Clues [Leeds], Ossie Bevan [Warrington] and Max Garbler [Saints]. The crowd were delighted with the brilliant football served up. Peter Henderson's pace was always something that a true rugby league supporter would pay to see and he certainly didn't let the crowd down showing his Olympic pace in the middle of the field in scoring two sparkling tries, both long distance efforts. The world's most exciting wingman, 'Bev' scored a brace of tries that were out of the top drawer. Lionel Cooper blasted over for one of his powerful tries and the tough Max Garbler exerted his power near the line to smash over. Throughout the game Arthur revelled in the freedom this festival game gave him. The crowd rose as one as in a strong burst he side stepped both Ken Gee and the even bigger Jack Booth, dummied Jacky Evans, who would never buy a dummy, and when being caught by Eric Hesketh, fed big Cooper who demolished the covering Great Britain forwards. Joe Phillips was his cool, distinguished self at full back and landed four super goals to give the antipodeans a well deserved 23 points. Great Britain responded and the silky smooth footballers, Jack Hilton and Russell Pepperell, scored beautiful tries from a long way out and the big men, Jack Booth and George Parsons crashed over from close range. The great Ernest Ward kicked four goals to give Great Britain a worthy 20 points but the finishing score of 23–20 to Australasia was well deserved and some great football sent the crowd home happy. For once Arthur and Ken Gee got through a game without fighting with each other as the Festival of Britain was all about goodwill towards men, just as Arthur and Ken liked it!

7

ARTHUR V EDOUARD PONSINET

Arthur, now in his 27th year, was in his prime. His learning curve into the British way of playing rugby league was now complete and his form, especially in big games, was outstanding. Arthur and his fiancée, Muriel Wood, had set a date to marry in 1952 and the big Aussie was considering what line of business to follow once married. Being a full time rugby league player would not be a permanent job so he started to contemplate an alternative livelihood to keep the couple in a good standard of living.

On the playing side, because of his outstanding leadership on the field, Arthur was appointed team captain. Leeds opened the league season with a good away win at Crown Flatt. The ground had been the graveyard of hopes for the Loiners so many times. Drew Turnbull had ended the previous season scoring 33 tries and Bruce Ryan had scored 25 tries. Both players crossed for good wingmen's tries with Bert Cook kicking two goals in this 10–0 win. Arthur missed this game and the following one (a five points all draw at the Barley Mow against Bramley). Turnbull again scored the Leeds touchdown and Cook obliged with the conversion. Arthur returned after a slight injury for the tough fixture at Wilderspool, Warrington but Leeds came off second best in a close 28–21 defeat, Turnbull again scoring a good try. Then two days later, Halifax beat Leeds at Headingley by 22–16 to make it a poor start to the league season with two defeats and a draw in the first four games. The young loose forward Geoff

Moore had been given a chance with both Arthur and Des Clarkson being indisposed in the early games. Also Leeds had signed Ken Ward, a very good utility back from Oldham.

The first leg of the Yorkshire Cup was played at Headingley against Bramley. Leeds took a handy 18–8 lead to the Barley Mow. The second leg was played nine days later as two home league games on 3rd and 8th September were fitted in. Batley were welcomed first to Headingley as Arthur had a change of second row partner as young Moore moved up to make way for Clarkson at loose forward. The result was a 17–10 win for Leeds. Leeds also won on 8th September as Workington Town were the visitors and made the long trip home as 15–12 losers. Back up the hill to Bramley went Leeds for the second leg of the County Cup and a convincing 25–9 win gave them an aggregate 43–17 gangway into round two. Arthur and Turnbull were among the try scorers at the Barley Mow. Turnbull recorded tries in seven of the first eight games of the season. Three days later Leeds travelled to Doncaster for the first time in their history (the Dons had been admitted into the league for the start of the 1951–1952 season). They were player-coached by the former Leeds favourite, Gareth Price, the free scoring centre and did remarkably well in their early days. But Leeds proved too strong for them on their first encounter winning 19–7 at the old ground surrounded by the greyhound track. Turnbull continued in his rich seam of form with two sparkling tries and Arthur chipped in with another beauty covering 30 yards in a super solo effort. Bradford Northern had been drawn in round two of the County Cup at Odsal, but Leeds first had to face a home game against Huddersfield, the strong, classy side from Fartown, where in a classical game of fast flowing rugby football a big crowd of over 27,000 were entertained to the full. Leeds matched everything the famous claret and gold jerseys threw at them in a thrilling end to end confrontation. The outcome was a fantastic 29–15 Leeds win with wonderful tries from Ken

Ward, Bruce Ryan, Des Clarkson, Frank Watson and big
Arthur (scoring in his third match on the trot). Bert Cook was
at his goal kicking best and landed seven successful shots. It
was on to the County Cup and Leeds faced Northern in a
game which included another fierce conflict in the Traill-
Clues vendetta. Another of Arthur's 'regular' opponents was
the late, great Trevor Foster who played for Bradford
Northern in this particular game. On numerous occasions
Trevor was asked, 'Who was the best forward you ever played
with or against?'

He answered every time, 'Without a doubt, Arthur Clues.
He could do everything, was superbly skilful, was tough and
was always a winner.'

Leeds won this bruising battle 14–13. What a cup tie!
Bruce Ryan scoring two tries, one off a massive Clues break
and run before sending Ryan hurtling over and Cook kicked
four good goals. Three days later Leeds walked through the
Odsal gates again, this time for a league game. Turnbull
scored two great tries to go with one try each from Dickie
Williams and Ken Ward. There were also three Cook goals
which gave Leeds another thrilling 18–9 win. Dewsbury
arrived at Headingley on 6th October to be beaten by 29–10.
This was just before the semi-final of the Yorkshire Cup
which brought those doughty cup fighters, Wakefield Trinity,
to Leeds. A total of 22,300 spectators turned out on Monday
8th October to witness a real cliff hanger of a semi-final. The
former international forward, Bill Hudson (who had played at
both Batley and Wigan) arrived at Belle Vue as pack leader
and captain but was missing from this match because of
suspension. His place was taken by the vastly experienced Jim
Higgins in the front row. The Leeds team was: Bert Cook;
Drew Turnbull, Bob Bartlett, Gordon Brown, Bruce Ryan;
Dickie Williams, Frank Watson; Bob McMaster, Arthur
Wood, Bill Hopper, Arthur Clues, Bernard Poole and Des
Clarkson. Wakefield had a mixture of youth and experience in

their line up. Their team was: Les Hirst; Johnny Duggan, Frank Mortimer, Don Froggett, Dennis Booker; Glyn Meredith, Arthur Fletcher; Jack Booth, Denny Horner, Jim Higgins, Derek Howes, Don Robinson and Reg Hughes. Standing at the head of the league table after winning six games consecutively, Leeds were a confident team with Arthur Clues so much in form, particularly after the thrilling one point win at Odsal in the previous round. Leeds had not won the Yorkshire Cup since 1937 and the presence of that mighty silver trophy had been sadly missed in the board room cabinet. 'This must be the year,' ran the thoughts of all at Leeds as the teams lined up on that Monday evening.

Referee Mr Adams of Hull, was held up in traffic and senior touch-judge, Mr W.I. Wraith, took over until Mr Adams' arrival. Hirst, the Wakefield full back, normally a centre, playing at number one because of the injury to the experienced Ernest Luckman, landed two early penalty goals to remind Leeds that this would be no easy walk through to the final. Leeds hooker, Arthur Wood, signed from Featherstone Rovers during the last close season as a replacement for Ken Kearney (who was returning home) was winning the ball two to one against a local Leeds man Denny Horner. Denny was a Burley Road lad who lived only a few hundred yards away from Headingley. Despite having plenty of ball play, Leeds struggled to dent the strong Trinity defence. Arthur Clues was at his outstanding best despite actually being thrown back twice from the Trinity line when looking to be an odds-on scorer. He was thrown back firstly by the 19 year old Don Robinson, then in a combined Les Hirst and Jim Higgins tackle. It was left in the capable hands of Dickie Williams who, accepting a pass some 30 yards out, set off on an explosive arched run that mesmerised the Trinity tacklers as the red haired stand off shot over to register a surprise try, Cook's conversion giving Leeds a one point advantage. Arthur Fletcher played well and was involved in most of the plays that Trinity threw at Leeds. Firstly his swift, accurate pass from the scrum base was collected by half back partner Meredith who dropped a smart goal. Then Fletcher drew two tacklers to himself and managed the perfect pass to get the speedster Duggan racing away down the side line. Duggan suddenly side stepped with a huge stride infield that sent both Cook and Turnbull covering the wrong way and the Trinity wingman raced in for a brilliant try, Hirst converting. Wakefield were now playing like champions and it seemed that the teams would change around with Trinity leading by six points. But Cook was given the opportunity to kick at goal in the final seconds of the half. He converted the penalty with a superb goal to end the half 7–11 to Wakefield.

In the second half, Trinity started to capitalise on their confident play as Fletcher, easily the best player, dropped a fine goal within a minute of the restart. Then, only a couple of minutes after Fetcher's shock two pointer, former Headingley Rugby Union flanker, Reg Hughes, picked up a ball some 50 yards out from the Leeds line and exploded into a gap in the Leeds defence. Surging past four tacklers, Hughes showed tremendous pace in his dash to the line for an exceptionally fine try, to which Hirst added the extra points. In front suddenly by 18–7, Trinity must have thought they were through but Cook replied with another great penalty goal. Then as the clock ticked away showing 11 minutes to play, Poole crashed over just inside the flag and Cook, in brilliant form with his boot, landed a monster goal from the touch line to make it 18–14 with still enough time for Leeds to win the semi-final. Seven minutes left and Bartlett was sent on a run to the line. As he approached Hirst he seemed to loose the ball forward but referee Adams called, 'Play on!' The ball rebounded off Hirst straight back into Bartlett's hands and he flashed over, wide out. Cook's kick, which surely would have given Leeds a County Cup final place, looked a winner all the way off the boot, but in the final few feet faded away and flicked the post on its way wide of the mark. Still there was time for Leeds to win. Trinity were now out on their feet as Dickie Williams made one of his trade mark bursts in mid field and passed to the supporting Arthur Clues only 10 yards from the Trinity line. Arthur shook off a crunching double tackle by Robinson and Hughes but staggered as he left the two would-be heroes behind. As he adjusted his position to take a low dive over the line, Hirst somehow managed to smother Arthur in a try saving tackle that grassed the big Aussie literally inches short of the line. As Hirst released his grip on Arthur for one final play the ball, Mr Adams blew for full time to end one of the most exciting games seen at Headingley in living memory. Despite losing in a major semi-final the crowd cheered both teams off the field, so intense had this cup tie been.

The following Saturday, Leeds made the trip across to Wigan's Central Park and took a heavy beating by the tough Lancashire men. Losing 44–5 was bad enough but they also lost the services of ace goal kicker Bert Cook with a reoccurrence of the shoulder injury that had dogged him for a season or two. He played only four further games that season, coming back and being let down again by the injury. In the next game, Bramley at Headingley, Leeds returned to the winning path with a 42–2 victory. Turnbull zoomed in for five tries and Cook's replacement, local lad Jimmy Dunn, landed eight goals. A good win at Parkside saw Leeds beat local rivals Hunslet 20–13, Arthur again delivering a real top game for this derby match. The following weekend both Arthur and the Leeds team were involved with Humberside. The Leeds team were at Headingley to play Hull Kingston Rovers and Arthur was at the Boulevard, playing for Other Nationalities against France.

The 3rd November 1951 was a cold day with a slight mist coming in off the mighty Humber Estuary. When the teams were printed in the Hull Daily Mail the knowledgeable Hull rugby league people looked immediately at the French second row to see if the tough policeman from Marseilles was included. The former boxing champion, Eduoard Ponsinet, was that second row forward and he was also the man that Arthur had badly injured with a terrible high tackle in Bordeaux on 10th December 1950. Ponsinet had come to play at the Boulevard and was ready to take on the big, tough Clues, who had caught him so badly in France almost one year before. This game had an aura that one could taste and feel. The atmosphere at the Boulevard crackled with expectation. Everyone present just knew that they were about to see a test level game and that something was about to happen. The game went into folklore as one of the hardest games ever seen at the Boulevard. Historians christened it, 'The Battle of the Boulevard.' It could so easily have been called, 'The Infamous War of the Boulevard.'

The teams lined up, Other Nationalities: Johnny Hunter [Huddersfield]; Brian Bevan [Warrington], Tony Paskins [Workington Town], Pat Devery [Huddersfield], Lionel Cooper [Huddersfield]; Peter Henderson [Huddersfield], Cec Kelly [Rochdale Hornets]; Bob McMaster [Leeds], Tom McKinney [Salford], John Mudge [Workington Town], Arthur Clues [Leeds], Jeff Burke [Leigh] and Dave Valentine [Huddersfield]. France: Puig-Aubert; R. Contrastin, J. Merquey, G. Comes, V. Cantoni; R. Duffort, J. Crespo; L. Mazon, M. Martin, P. Bartoletti, E. Brousse, E. Ponsinet and F. Montrocolis. The referee was the usually very strict, Mr George Phillips of Widnes.

The Other Nationalities won the toss and decided to kick to the Frenchmen. This was an old ploy used by any team playing the French by which, giving the ball to the French, the kicking team could knock seven bells out of them as early as possible, believing that by doing this the French would surrender and the game would be easier. But Puig-Aubert and Eduoard Ponsinet had sprung a trap which caught the Other Nationalities when as Cec Kelly kicked off, Puig-Aubert returned a 65 yard spiralling touch finder. The game was only one minute old when the first scrum took place. On the first drive in of the game, Arthur was the ball carrier. Ponsinet charged straight at Arthur and swung a huge stiff arm tackle that caught the big Aussie across the eye and temple. Arthur went down as if shot. He was out cold! Arthur was 'blowing bubbles'. His head and eyes were rolling all over the place he was concussed and bleeding heavily from a severe cut to the eyebrow. Arthur gamely tried to stand up but slid back down and the physio drew the attention of Mr Bill Fallowfield, the Other Nationalities officer in charge, to signal that he was bringing Arthur off. Four forwards, McMaster, Mudge, Burke and McKinney carried Arthur to the old dressing room steps and transferred him onto a stretcher. He was then taken into the dressing room for the doctor to examine him. The doctor sent him straight to the Hull Royal Infirmary to be hospitalised. Because of his early success against the fearsome Clues, Ponsinet took on the remainder of the Aussies in the pack and in fact had serious punch ups with all the other five forwards. The last straw was Ponsinet's assault on the tough Jeff Burke which left the Aussie with a broken nose. At this Mr Phillips told him to, 'Get off, now,' which he did to the jeers of the totally entertained 18,000 Hull crowd.

Ponsinet certainly left his mark on international matches in that era and in their first clash when Arthur flattened the big Frenchman, Dave Valentine, a great player and a hard man, said that he hoped Arthur had, 'Killed the bugger,' for the amount of stick he was handing out. But Ponsinet lived on and returned to even the score with big Arthur. Years later when talking about the Battle of the Boulevard Arthur loved to give his version of the incident.

'I knew the big bastard would want to get even but I never

thought it would be so f****** early,' he would say.

Despite some incident-strewn periods of the game it was indeed memorable for the brilliant football played, mainly by the French. Everything good about their game stemmed from their ability to support and the skill of being able to find that support with unbelievable passes from impossible angles. They were magic when in this mood. The Other Nationalities though had an ace up their sleeve in the massive frame of their captain and legendary wingman, Lionel Cooper. Using every ounce of his immense power and strength and every bit of his vast experience, Cooper stormed over for a wonderful hat trick of tries and his long time pal and Huddersfield playing partner, Pat Devery, kicked four great goals to give Other Nationalities a memorable 17–14 win. The exciting French outfit scored two long range tries from V. Cantoni, their long striding wingman and the big prop P. Bartoletti. Puig-Aubert kicked superbly to land four goals in attaining their 14 points tally.

So the Battle of the Boulevard went into the history books, but the Clues-Ponsinet vendetta was not over just yet, there was one further chapter of this feud to come.

Whilst Arthur was being nursed at the infirmary, Leeds were beating Hull Kingston Rovers 33–22. This was thanks to another super hat trick of tries by Drew Turnbull and two tries by Arthur Staniland, plus six goals by Dunn, playing once more in place of Bert Cook. Arthur naturally missed the next game, a trip to Thrum Hall, following his confrontation with Monsieur Ponsinet. Halifax won the encounter 18–2. He also missed the game against New Zealand on 17th November at Headingley which the tourists won 19–4. Arthur was back for the trip to Lawkholme Lane to take on Keighley and was a try scorer in the 12–5 win.

On 1st December 1951, Other Nationalities took on a very strong Welsh national side at Abertillery before another meagre crowd of 3,386. Arthur packed down with his old mate Harry Bath in a side that showed only one change from the infamous Boulevard game. Jeff Burke moved up into the field side prop position allowing Bath to come alongside Arthur in the second row. The side was: Johnny Hunter; Brian Bevan, Tony Paskins, Pat Devery, Lionel Cooper; Peter Henderson, Cec Kelly; Jeff Burke, Tom McKinney, John Mudge, Arthur Clues, Harry Bath and Dave Valentine. The Welsh team was: Jacky Evans [Hunslet]; Mel Hunt [Cardiff], Les Williams, Vivian Harrison [St Helens], Terry Cook [Halifax]; Dickie Williams [Leeds], Billy Banks [Huddersfield]; Ossie Phillips [Swinton], Frank Osmond [Swinton], Elwyn Gwyther [Belle Vue Rangers], Doug Phillips [Belle Vue Rangers], Ted Ward [Cardiff] and Ray Cale [St Helens].

Ted Ward, the former Wigan centre and 1946 tourist had moved down to Cardiff to be player-coach at the new club and was operating in the second row in this game. The Welsh pack was particularly strong with two excellent Belle Vue Rangers included. One of the Rangers was big Doug Phillips who had clashed with Arthur on several occasions both on the 1946 tour and in club football since his arrival at Headingley. The other Ranger was the tough, solid Elwyn Gwyther who had toured with the 1950 side. Ray Cale was a big, strong experienced forward at number 13 and Wales were always hard to beat, especially in the principality. This time the Other Nationalities had played together more and had formed understandings about each other's play far better than in October 1949 when the two sides met for the first time. Naturally, Doug Phillips, Ted Ward and Elwyn Gwyther tested Arthur's resolve after his encounter with big Edouard but early on, big Doug found himself on the seat of his pants after meeting Arthur head on. The combined overseas side was filled with world class three-quarters. Paskins and Devery were, at this time, arguably the finest centre partnership in the world and their wingmen were definitely the two best in the universe! Both Bevan and Cooper, the rapier and the broadsword, were in a class of their own. Bevan, the will-o-the-wisp danger man could score a try from his own try line with ease. His swerve on the run and his quick change of direction completely ruined any cover tackler and his pace was outstanding. Cooper, the 15 stones plus monster was all aggression and power. He used his hips as a hand-off, waiting with perfect timing until the tackler was about to take him, then bang, he would hit the tackler with a sway of his hips sending him head over heels. Lionel had pace too, enough to escape the covering forwards and score wonderful, memorable tries that people lucky enough to watch him play, still talk about. The referee, once again the brilliant Charlie Appleton, knew how to handle games like these and allowed play to continue without the stop-start scenario we see sometimes today.

The small Welsh crowd was thrilled by the Other Nationalities backs and indicative of the fantastic ball handling skills of both sides, all nine tries scored in this classic were registered by backs. Bevan scored two magnificent long range tries as did Pat Devery. Cooper, released by Devery inside his own half, blitzed his way down field, like a runaway dump truck, to walk in under the bar and Tony Paskins supported a magnificent side stepping break by Arthur to accept his final pass and stride over majestically. Wales had their say in the pulsating game with Mel Hunt, Les Williams and Dickie Williams all scoring terrific solo tries. The goal kicking was shared out with Devery and Harry Bath kicking one each for the visitors and Ted Ward kicking one for Wales, as the Other Nationalities won 22–11.

The main feature of this game was the work, as a second row partnership, of Clues and Bath. It was as if they were made to play together, each one knowing the play of the other and sometimes seeming to have a premonition of the moves of one another. The Clues-Bath partnership slid into the folklore of the game, as if it had been destined to do so. This owed much to their joint performance in this international match in Abertillery. The Welsh crowd were experts in reading the skills of rugby football, either Union or League, and Harry and Arthur enchanted them. Tries from brilliant three-quarters were the icing on the cake but the bread and butter was their forward play. The individual breaks, interpassing, support of each other and their double tackling was a joy to watch. Everything about Arthur Clues and Harry Bath was international standard and their combined play was devastating.

Harry Bath returned home in 1957 to play for St George and earned the nickname of 'The Old Fox'. He went into coaching later and was tremendously successful, winning the Grand Final and coaching Australia in the World Cups of 1968 and 1970. He retired in 1981 as coach of Balmain. The Australian public never saw the best of Arthur Clues. Sure, he played in test football for his country and was their outstanding forward in the 1946 tests but his brilliant years as the best second row forward in the world were spent in the UK. It is only the keenest of Australian supporters who genuinely can say, 'Yes, Clues was the best.' If he had returned to Australia as a player he would, no doubt, have been hailed by the Aussie club and international supporters but the big man decided to spend the remainder of his life in and around the city of Leeds. Leeds considered him to be the finest forward of all time.

On the day that Other Nationalities beat Wales, Leeds beat Featherstone Rovers at Headingley 18–8, Turnbull registering another two tries. The next three games for Leeds were all against Humberside teams. Leeds faced Hull Kingston Rovers at Craven Park and were beaten by 19–13. The week after, Leeds played at the Boulevard where the Loiners were no match for Hull FC and lost 25–15. Arthur was not in the side that played at Hull Kingston Rovers but he played in the next two games (the defeat at the Boulevard) and against Hull FC again on 22nd December at Headingley. The result at Headingley was also a bad one as Leeds were outplayed by the big Hull FC pack and lost 22–10. One month before, Leeds lost the services of excellent loose forward, Des Clarkson, who was transferred to Halifax. This left the club a touch short of class back row forwards. This problem was exposed on Christmas Day when Leeds travelled to Mount Pleasant, Batley to be beaten 15–7.

Arthur was suspended for two matches and missed the Batley game. The Leeds team looked a strange affair with Denis Murphy, normally a second row or loose forward, at full back and goal kicker. The pack looked unusual in the shape of McMaster, Wood, Kendrick, Poole, Scholes and Moore. Denis Scholes had played on the wing for Hull Kingston Rovers on 3rd November 1951 against Leeds at Headingley when he'd scored four tries. He was a second row forward who had played on the wing because of injury to the regular Hull KR wingmen but was not a regular first team player. Leeds signed him on the strength of his four tries. Having good backs was of little use if the pack was not going forward and the excellent Turnbull, Bartlett, Brown, Staniland, Ken Ward and Frank Watson's skill was wasted because of the forwards' weaknesses. Turnbull crossed again for a try against Batley as he had done four days earlier against Hull FC at home.

Boxing Day saw Wakefield Trinity visit Headingley and with a few changes, Leeds were a different outfit. The changes had Harold Oddy, a local signing from Hawksworth Old Boys on debut in the centre partnering Ted Verrenkamp who was on the wing for the injured Turnbull. Bruce Ryan was on the other wing for Andrew Staniland with Johnny Feather at scrum half for Frank Watson. Alan Horsfall hooked for Arthur Wood. The result was an outstanding

30–11 win for Leeds. The final game of 1951 was another let down when, with Staniland on the wing for Verrenkamp, Leeds lost 16–7 to the old derby enemy, Hunslet, at Headingley.

Arthur returned against one of the hardest sides in the league, Warrington at home. He was straight back into the form that made him the league's most respected forward. A superb facet of Arthur's game was that he could hit great form immediately after any length of time off. He did this in this Warrington game. Despite his alliance with Harry Bath in representative football, Arthur always wanted to better his Aussie counterpart when they met at club level. They had real punch ups, no holds barred and this game was no exception. Bath would often say, when discussing Arthur, 'That Cluesy was a crazy bastard, never knew when he was beat. He was tough too and on top of all that the bastard could play.' Harry Bath's comments about Clues had the word 'respect' running through them. Leeds beat Warrington that day 22–3 with Arthur again outstanding as pack leader.

The bubble burst the following week when the fledgling Doncaster came to Headingley and produced the shock of the league season by beating Leeds 11–6. This game saw the introduction of an Australian centre who would become one of the club's greatest captains in years to come, Keith McLellan. Keith and Bruce Ryan scored tries for Leeds in this defeat.

Wednesday 23rd January 1952 heralded a new concept in international football when a British Empire XIII took on the New Zealand touring team at Stamford Bridge, Chelsea, in a Festival of Britain game. The Empire team comprised a mixture of Great Britain players and Other Nationalities players and was: Jack Cunliffe [Wigan]; Brian Bevan [Warrington], Trevor Allan [Leigh], Ernest Ward [Bradford Northern], Lionel Cooper [Huddersfield]; Jacky Broome

[Wigan], Albert Pepperell [Workington Town]; Frank Barton [Wigan], Tom McKinney [Salford], Alan Prescott [St Helens], Arthur Clues [Leeds], Harry Bath [Warrington] and Dave Valentine [Huddersfield]. The Kiwis selected a test level team for this prestigious event and the side was: D. White; J. Edwards, W. Hough, C. Eastlake, W. Sorenson; D. Barchard, J. Haig; C. Johnson, W. Davidson, D. Blanchard, C. McBride, D. Richards-Jolley and A. Atkinson. The referee was once again the reliable Mr Charlie Appleton of Warrington.

The result was a rousing 26–2 win for the Empire team. The foundation for the win was laid by the Empire forward strength. The twin threat of Clues and Bath was far too much for the Kiwis to handle and with thunderous running by Barton and Prescott and the smart linking of Valentine, Pepperell and Broome with Ernest Ward and Trevor Allan, allowed Bevan and Cooper to dominate the touch lines. 'Bev' went in for his single try from 60 yards and Cooper rampaged over for a superb hat trick of tries from 20, 40 and 55 yards in that order. Trevor Allan and Dave Valentine added a try apiece and Ernest Ward landed four goals. For New Zealand, Don White landed a penalty goal. Arthur had a rumble with big Charlie McBride after the Kiwi second rower had flattened Harry Bath off the ball.

Arthur's international CV was beginning to accumulate the prestige he deserved because of his consistency in the week to week games he turned out for Leeds. Selection for Other Nationalities, The Rest of the League and the British Empire, added to his caps for Australia and New South Wales. This gave the big man just about every selection honour available.

Returning for a game at Fartown, Arthur played against his mate from the Other Nationalities, Dave Valentine, the Huddersfield loose forward. The pair had a battle royal on a mud strewn pitch. The power of Lionel Cooper told when Huddersfield beat Leeds 30–10. Arthur missed the next three matches. They were Wigan at home which Leeds lost 17–7 and also two legs of the Challenge Cup first round against Hull Kingston Rovers. The first leg was played at Headingley and with the aid of five tries by Bruce Ryan and four by Drew Turnbull, Leeds took a lead of 44–14 to Craven Park the following week. Here a hard fought game ended in a narrow Leeds win by 5–3, giving a 49–19 aggregate win to the Loiners. York at Clarence Street was the next venue for Leeds and Arthur returned at loose forward, locking a strange looking Leeds pack of Nutting, a very young Bernard Prior, Hopper, Scholes, Poole and Clues. York beat Leeds 13–6. The Leeds backs were Bert Cook (still unfit), Staniland, McLellan, Oddy and Ryan.

The second round of the Challenge Cup brought Oldham to Headingley. Arthur had been injured at York which kept him out of the side but a closely fought cup tie ended with a good Leeds victory of 12–9 and a tough trip to Leigh in the vital third round of the cup. Leeds beat York in the league at Leeds 21–3. Arthur scored a fine try in his first game for Leeds as a prop forward.

Excitement grew as the team prepared for the stiff cup game at Hilton Park. Leigh were a strong cup tie team, hard to beat on their own tight ground and full of local lads who would die for the club. The Leeds team for the cup tie was: Dunn; Turnbull, Bartlett, Brown, McLellen; Ward, Feather; McMaster, Wood, Clues, Poole, Scholes and Moore. The Leigh team was: Jim Ledgard; Ted Kerwick, Trevor Allan, Norman Harris, Billy Kindon; Ken Baxter, Harry Green; Jeff Burke, Walt Tabern, Harry Edden, Charlie Pawsey, Peter Foster, Bill McFarlane. A Drew Turnbull try and Jimmy Dunn goal was not enough to win this hard cup tie as Leigh scored nine points in a hard earned victory.

Arthur was back in the second row for the next game, at home to Bradford Northern, when the big crowd was entertained by a 16 all draw in a very exciting league game. Out of the Challenge Cup, the Leeds season stuttered to its

usual end with a drubbing at Belle Vue where Wakefield
Trinity ran up a huge 34–8 win with Arthur back at prop. This
was followed by a close run match away at Workington Town
where Leeds were beaten by 10–9 with Arthur again moved
back into the second row. Castleford at home was club's next
fixture which ended in a tight 12–9 win for Leeds in a game
that saw the debut of one of the Loiners finest half backs, Jeff
Stevenson. The following day, Leeds travelled to Post Office
Road, Featherstone to take on the Rovers to be beaten 16–5,
this time with Stevenson at stand off half. In their fifth game
in 13 days, Leeds beat Castleford at Wheldon Road 18–7 and
ended the league season in style with a big 38–13 win over
Keighley at Headingley in the final game.

Arthur missed the last two games as he was selected again
for the Other Nationalities to play England at Central Park,
Wigan on Wednesday 23rd April 1952. A crowd of almost
20,000 turned out to see a tremendous free flowing game
with 11 tries scored by some of the games finest players. The
overseas team had Ted Verrenkamp in at stand off half and
Harry Bath showing his versatility with a grand display at
blind side prop. Arthur was right behind his mate in the pack
at blind side second row forward. Just after half time, after
one almighty push by the England forwards in the scrum,
Harry Bath pulled Arthur and complained that he was slow
out of the pack to cover the blind side and that also he was
just leaning on in the scrum and not pushing his normal
weight. 'Here Cluesy,' said Harry, 'Give us a bit more push in
the scrum yer lazy bastard.'

Arthur was most apologetic and replied, 'It's me f******
leg mate, it's crook.' It turned out he had broken a bone in his
ankle. The teams that lined up that day were, Other
Nationalities: Johnny Hunter [Huddersfield]; Brian Bevan
[Warrington], Tony Paskins [Workington Town], Trevor Allan
[Leigh], Lionel Cooper [Huddersfield]; Ted Verrenkamp
[Leeds], Cec Kelly [Rochdale Hornets]; Bob McMaster

[Leeds], Tom McKinney [Salford], Harry Bath [Warrington], John Mudge [Workington Town], Arthur Clues [Leeds] and Dave Valentine [Huddersfield]. The England side was: Jimmy Ledgard [Leigh]; Dick Cracknell [Huddersfield], Dougie Greenall [St Helens], Ernest Ward [Bradford Northern], Frank Castle [Barrow]; Willie Horne [Barrow], Ted Toohey [Barrow]; Alan Prescott [St Helens], Alvin Ackerley [Halifax], Frank Barton [Wigan], Nat Silcock [Wigan], Charlie Pawsey [Leigh] and Billy Ivison [Workington Town]. The referee was Mr T. Armitage [Huddersfield].

Despite Harry Bath being in the front row, he and Arthur continued with their excellent partnership until big Arthur's injury. 'Bev' scored another wonderful brace of tries on the ground at Central Park where he scored many great tries in his long career. Trevor Allan also registered a couple of excellent tries and Harry Bath kicked three fine goals. All England's points came from their backs. Dick Cracknell scored two tries, as did the Barrow flyer, Frank Castle. Jimmy Ledgard, Willie Horne and Dougie Greenall scored a try apiece, with Ledgard scoring two tries and Horne scoring three, adding the goal kicks. The final score was England 31 Other Nationalities 18.

8

MARRIED AND
SETTLING DOWN

Breaking a bone in his ankle was bad enough but Arthur was due to marry Muriel very shortly and indeed, hobbled down the aisle with his new bride on his arm and his leg in plaster of Paris.

It was about this time that Arthur opened his sport outfitters shop in Woodhouse Lane (the main road into the city of Leeds from the North). He was warned by the famous Yorkshire and England opening batsman Herbert Sutcliffe that his business would fold within six weeks. Herbert Sutcliffe had conducted the same type of business for many years from prestigious city centre premises. Arthur actually lasted longer than Herbert's estimated six weeks. In fact he operated for almost 30 years. Eventually he changed his showroom from his established Woodhouse Lane site to the new purpose built Merrion Street complex in the city centre where his business flourished. His open attitude was ready made for the warm and friendly greetings he generated when calling into the shop. At this time I played for the Leeds junior under 16 side, Headingley Juniors. I called into his shop to buy a pair of boot laces and was served by Arthur as if I had bought the shop out. He not only sold me the laces but asked me about who I played for, what position I played and actually asked how I tied my boots to play in a match. He showed me how he tied his and I did the same for the remainder of my playing career. He was a superb advert for the old fashioned shop salesman and because he was Arthur Clues everyone wanted to be served by him. His personality was immense. When he spoke to an individual it was as though there were only two people in the whole shop (the place was usually crowded). It was the same when Clues was playing rugby. His superb ability and charisma seemed to make watching him a very private thing. Somehow only the individual and Arthur were in the ground allowing the spectators to be enveloped into his game. It was a wonderful feeling.

The 1952–1953 season saw the arrival at Headingley of one of the game's biggest ever signings from the 15-a-side game. This was when the Leeds club brought the 'Golden Boy' of Welsh Rugby Union, Lewis Jones, 'up north'. Two additional good Welsh players were added to the Leeds squad when the tall, elegant Ralph Morgan was signed from Swinton and the tough front rower, Elwyn Gwyther, came to Leeds from Belle Vue Rangers. Leeds also introduced two young local players during this season and both went on to become excellent servants to the club. One was Clifford Last, a Middleton lad who joined Leeds after the club had run a trial game at Headingley with selected juniors invited to play. The other developed into a fine wing three-quarter and played at Wembley for Leeds in the cup winning side of 1957 when Barrow were beaten 9–7. He was George Broughton and he was signed from Castleford to take the place of the excellent Bruce Ryan who had returned home to Australia. Cliff Last remembers Arthur with the fondness of a youngster playing alongside a legend. Cliff was 17 when he made his first team debut against Bramley. 'He was wonderful to play alongside,' said Cliff, 'I remember as a 17 year old, playing in my first outing in the first team. Naturally I was as nervous as a kitten and I was up against one of my childhood heroes in Sammy Newbound, the former Hunslet forward, then playing for Bramley. Sammy was a big, tough man who had won the Mr Yorkshire bodybuilding title as a young man. He was beautifully built and could use himself in a fight. Arthur was always talking in the dressing room before a match and he would do the rounds of the youngsters in the team, reassuring them and filling them with confidence. He was brilliant at that. He was in his playing kit and he came across to me and sat by my side. "Cliffy," he said to me, "just play your normal game. Don't worry about big Sammy, I'll look after you kid. Okay Cliffy?" I said, "thanks Arthur."

'During the game I made a half break and big Sammy, doing his job like a good pro, gave me a smack as I passed the ball to the support. It didn't hurt really, not as much as I expected but as I regained my feet, Arthur ran past Sammy and no one saw what happened except Sammy dropped to the ground as if pole axed. The referee stopped the game and signalled the physio on. Sammy came round and was being helped to his feet as Arthur stood near him. "Keep away from young Cliffy, Sam or they will take longer to bring you round next time," he whispered in Sammy's ear. He was as good as his word, he looked after me until he thought I was ready to look after myself. He was a great bloke, Arthur.'

Arthur and Cliff between them helped save the life of a forward who had recently been transferred to Leeds from Batley, Tommy Shirtliffe. In a first leg Challenge Cup game against Shirtliffe's former club at Headingley, Shirtliffe suddenly collapsed whist on the field during the game. Arthur and Cliff ran to him and found he was in a bad way suffering an epileptic fit. Both Arthur and Cliff tended to him whilst the physio sprinted on and revived the stricken forward. Tommy played only four games for Leeds and had to retire after this dangerous attack. But for Arthur and Cliff's swift action, Tommy may well have died on the field.

The season began with a home game against the team from Barrow-in-Furness on 23rd August 1952. In a tough encounter Barrow won 3–2. For the first time in quite a few years the Leeds club had local youngsters in line for first team places. The full back position though was causing concern as the reliable and experienced Bert Cook was still unable to throw off the chronic shoulder injury that had plagued him for a few seasons. The club tried several players in the number one jersey without finding the right man. Morgan, Dunn, Denis Murphy, Woodhead and Cook himself all played at full back in the first 12 games of the season which was not conducive to building up a regular winning side. Other youngsters were to be added to the Leeds' first team pool, wingmen Raynor, Lynn and Garbutt and back row forward, Cliff Last. Bert Cook returned for the next two games. Leeds won both games. The games were Keighley away 19–10 (to Leeds) and the first leg of the Yorkshire Cup playing Hull FC away, 8–7 (to Leeds). Cook kicked five goals against Keighley and four goals against Hull FC.

Arthur had hit his form from the first game. Against Dewsbury at Headingley he was outstanding with a glorious try in the 37–9 win. On Friday 5th September, Hull FC came to Headingley in the second leg of the County Cup. Leeds held a one point advantage from the first leg but in front of a very healthy 18,000 crowd they could not hold the big, young, virile black and white pack. In a hard fought match the Leeds side lost 10–2 giving Hull FC the round by an aggregate of 17–10. The next day Leeds travelled to the Watersheddings to face Oldham. Playing a robust type of game the Rough'yeds beat a Leeds team playing their fourth game in eight days 21–10. Hunslet were defeated at Headingley, 21–12, with Drew Turnbull scoring four tries. Despite two more tries by Turnbull and one each by Arthur and Harold Oddy, Leeds lost the next game 29–22 at Warrington. Leeds played Oldham at home and Barrow away and lost both games. The scores were 7–4 to Oldham and 21–4 to Barrow. The hard Barrow side were brilliantly led by the master Willie Horne.

Arthur did get back on the winning path on 18th October when he was selected once more to play in the second row with Harry Bath for the Other Nationalities against England at Fartown, Huddersfield. The referee was the great Mr Ron Gelder of Wakefield and over 20,500 spectators watched another tremendous game. England had a strong side on view and played a well balanced team. They were: Jimmy Ledgard [Leigh]; Jim Lewthwaite [Barrow], Ron Ryder [Warrington], Ernest Ward [Bradford Northern], Frank Castle [Barrow]; Ken Dean [Halifax], Ted Toohey [Barrow]; Alan Prescott [St Helens], Alvin Ackerley [Halifax], Mick Scott [Hull FC], Charlie Pawsey [Leigh], Bob Ryan [Warrington] and Billy Blan [Wigan]. The Other Nationalities were almost as ever with Johnny Hunter [Huddersfield]; Brian Bevan [Warrington], Tony Paskins [Workington], Pat Devery [Huddersfield], Lionel Cooper [Huddersfield]; Peter Henderson [Huddersfield], Cec Kelly [Wigan]; John Daly [Featherstone Rovers], Tom McKinney [Salford], John Mudge [Workington Town], Harry Bath [Warrington], Arthur Clues [Leeds] and Dave Valentine [Huddersfield].

English spectators who remember Arthur Clues and Harry Bath in this game still wax lyrical about the way these two magnificent forwards played together. With Dave Valentine at loose forward, this must have been the classiest and toughest back three ever to have been seen in the game in this country. All three men combined to inflict a heavy defeat on England, with high power running and handling that had the big crowd in raptures and howling for more. So dominant were this back row that Brian Bevan literally walked over for four tries after sets of brilliant play by Bath, Clues and Valentine. Lionel Cooper powered in for one of his specials and Peter Henderson added a brace of tries simply by following Arthur and Harry. Bath also landed two goals and Pat Devery kicked three. The result was a crunching 31–12 win for the overseas team.

While Arthur was tearing the England team apart at Fartown. His Leeds team mates were beating Hull Kingston Rovers at Headingley 21–10. The following week, with Arthur back in the second row, Leeds beat York at Clarence Street 20–10. Dewsbury at Crown Flatt was a harder proposition and Leeds were beaten 18–7.

The big day finally happened on Saturday 8th November 1952 when Lewis Jones played his first game for Leeds in the 56–7 victory over Keighley. Jones played at full back and kicked seven goals. Arthur scored two tries in this big win and the team on that memorable day was: Jones; Turnbull, McLellan, Ward, Brown; Verrenkamp, Stevenson; Horsfall, Wood, Gwyther, Clues, Poole and Moore. Leeds beat Doncaster away 14–10 in the following game.

Australia played at Headingley the following week. Arthur missed the game against his fellow countrymen as he was playing against France at the Stade Velodrome in Marseilles on Sunday 23rd November for the Other Nationalities. Monsieur Ponsinet was not playing, which was understandable, as memories were long and tempers could be very short when one player owed another player one on account. The French side was a good one: Puig-Aubert; M. Bellan, J. Merquey, O. Lespes, G. Benausse; C. Teisseire, J. Crespo, F. Rinaldi, M. Martin, P. Bartoletti, H. Berthomieu, G. Delaye and R. Perez. The Other Nationalities side had one enforced change from the side which beat England so convincingly. Tommy Lynch, the great Kiwi centre from the Halifax club, came in at number three for the injured Tony Paskins. The Other Nationalities side was: Hunter; Bevan, Tommy Lynch, Devery, Cooper; Henderson, Kelly; Daly, McKinney, Mudge, Clues, Bath and Valentine. The overseas side scored seven tries. Bevan scored two tries, Cooper, Devery, Henderson, Kelly and Valentine all scored a try each. Harry Bath kicked four goals as the Other Nationalities recorded a 29–10 win before a crowd of 18,000. France scored two tries from J. Merquey and two Puig-Aubert goals. Again the overseas pack was devastating. Daley and Mudge took on the donkey work, Tom McKinney won the ball two to one and Clues, Bath and Valentine were massive players as, once more, the backs had a field day.

The day before this international game took place, Leeds faced the 1952 Australian touring Kangaroos at Headingley and the Aussies gave Leeds a lesson in support play and top class finishing to win 45–4. The week after, with Arthur at loose forward, Leeds went to Fartown and achieved a win against a strong Huddersfield side 27–21. Bert Cook came back for this game and kicked six goals.

The 6th December saw Warrington visit Headingley. Leeds were on top form with Arthur again leading the way. People said that Arthur always played to his best ability when Harry Bath was in the opposition. Well Bath was in the Warrington team that day but was totally eclipsed by a rampant Arthur who, in the 34–12 win scored three tries. Leeds played Hull FC twice in two weeks. The first game was at the Boulevard on 13th December where Leeds lost 14–7. Then Leeds played them again on 20th December at Headingley with Leeds winning 23–8. Arthur romped 25 yards for one of his special tries.

It was a productive Christmas for Leeds as they beat: Batley at home on 25th December, 20–16; Wakefield Trinity at Belle Vue, 27–9 on 26th December; and Featherstone Rovers at home on 27th December, 20–5. These were three hard games played in three days. After this came three bad defeats on the trot: Halifax at Thrum Hall on New Years Day, 22–2; Wakefield Trinity at home, 19–9; and Bradford Northern at Odsal, 34–5. Leeds beat their old enemy Hunslet at Headingley 15–10, but following this, a 10–5 win at Batley proved costly to Leeds as during the game Lewis Jones suffered a broken arm that ended his season. Lewis Jones was a tremendous player, the 'Golden Boy' of Welsh rugby union who possessed all the skills of Rugby Football and then some. In his book, King of Rugger, Lewis pays compliment to Arthur as a great player and a wonderful captain who led from the front. He also tells of how Arthur went out of his way to help him settle into rugby league when he first arrived at Leeds.

The Challenge Cup rolled around again and Leeds had drawn the hard cup fighters and old enemies, Wakefield Trinity in the two legs of the first round. Before this game, Leeds had to play a tough league game at Headingley against Bradford Northern. In the hard fought game, the Clues-Traill vendetta again surfaced and a running battle between the two started at kick off and continued to the end of the game. Bradford won the match 10–3 and the game ended with an ugly incident at the St Michaels Lane end, under the posts. Bradford were home and dry with a score of 10–0 in their favour. Arthur was playing at loose forward and supported a Jeff Stevenson break. As he'd been put into the clear, he headed for the posts. Caught about a yard short by two Bradford tacklers, Arthur used his tremendous strength to force himself over the line with a final surge. As he did so and laid on the ground, two Bradford forwards arrived simultaneously, and dived on top of Arthur. It happened quickly. As the referee awarded the try, Arthur jumped up from the ground, his face covered in blood and made a beeline for Ken Traill. Several Leeds players helped control Arthur as he was determined to have it out with Traill. With the goal kick missed in the commotion and players still trying to calm Arthur down, the referee blew for time and the Bradford players escorted Traill to the dressing room. The Leeds team, almost to a man, stayed out on the field with Arthur until the Bradford team had disappeared into the pavilion. The injury to Arthur was a deep cut above his eyebrow and in a report in the local newspaper, Arthur said it had felt like a boot had kicked him whilst he was prostrate on the grass.

Because of the melee after the Clues try, no one noticed that the referee had sent Arthur off after he had blown for time. Arthur was said to have thrown a punch at Traill before the players split up the feuding pair.

As the cup tie with Wakefield was held the following Saturday, Arthur could play as the disciplinary committee sat on the Monday after the Wakefield cup tie. Arthur played with stitches in his eyebrow at Belle Vue and had a good game in a healthy 33–9 victory for Leeds. The disciplinary committee gave Arthur a two match ban, creating a precedent of suspending a player for an offence committed after the end of a game whilst still on the field of play. The suspension meant that Arthur would miss the second leg cup tie at Headingley and the league match at Bramley the week after.

Leeds beat Wakefield again in the second leg of the cup tie 32–9 giving Leeds a 65–18 aggregate winning score. Leeds also defeated Bramley 28–0 at Barley Mow, putting Leeds in a confident mood to take on the dangerous Widnes at Headingley in round two of the Challenge Cup. Drew Turnbull led the way to a good 26–17 win over the 'Chemics' by scoring five superb tries, again building confidence to make the tough trip to Warrington at Wilderspool in the crucial third round. Doncaster were defeated at Headingley in the league 42–11, then came the Warrington cup tie.

The former Wigan great, Cec Mountford, had signed as player-manager-coach for the 'Wire'. Along with a strong pack including Bob Ryan, Jim Featherstone and Harry Bath and some excellent backs including Gerry Helme, Ron Ryder and Brian Bevin, the team proved far too strong for Leeds and won the encounter handsomely 25–8. Warrington went out to St Helens in the semi-final and Huddersfield beat Wigan in the other semi-final to go on to play what became known as 'Ramsden's' final when young Peter Ramsden won the Lance

Todd Trophy on his 19th birthday in Huddersfield's mighty win.

Leeds usually lost matches after coming out of the Challenge Cup but this time they continued the league fixtures with a series of wins. In fact Leeds only lost one game after the semi-final until the end of the season. First came York at home, with Turnbull scoring another four tries. York were beaten 33–19. Next Leeds played Halifax at home (beaten 19–10). On Good Friday 3rd April, Leeds beat Castleford 22–10 at Headingley. On 4th April Featherstone Rovers beat Leeds at Post Office Road 28–13. On Easter Monday 6th April, Castleford played host to Leeds at Wheldon Road and Leeds won 23–2. On 7th April (Leeds' fourth game in five days) they beat Bramley at Headingley 31–8. Drew Turnbull scored four tries against Bramley bringing his total, including the York game, to 13 tries in 5 games. This game also saw the debut of the excellent local lad, Cliff Last, who registered a goal kick in this big win. During the game against Featherstone away, Bert Cook damaged his shoulder again and unknown to anyone, would represent Leeds in only one further game before moving on to coach Keighley. Arthur missed the Castleford away game with a thigh strain. Despite this he still had the remarkable record of missing only eight games out of the 43 played by the club in the 1952–1953 season. As club captain over several seasons Arthur had, once again, shown tremendous club loyalty and durability.

The final two league matches were victories against Huddersfield (12–5) at home and Hull Kingston Rovers at Craven Park (28–7). Drew Turnbull scored two tries, one against Huddersfield and one against Hull Kingston Rovers to bring his try tally for the season to 35 tries in 22 games.

Arthur, although dreadfully disappointed by failure once more in the Challenge Cup, had one of his favourite big representative games to play before the season's end. The

Other Nationalities were joint top of the European international league with England on four points with Wales two points behind. The Other Nationalities had a far better points average than any other team. If the Welshmen wanted the international championship, they would have to beat the overseas team by a big score. The two teams met for the decider on 15th April at Warrington. This game should have been a home fixture for Wales but because of the small crowds watching the game in the principality it was played at Wilderspool.

Other Nationalities were welcomed back by the brilliant Cec Mountford. The teams lined up before a disappointing crowd of 8,500 spectators but the 'stay at homes' had some justification as it poured down before and throughout the game, making the pitch difficult. Wales selected a strong side in one final effort to steal the Jean Galia Trophy as outright winners of the European International Championship. The Dragons side was: Jack Evans [Hunslet]; Dai Bevan [Wigan], Les Williams [Hunslet], Norman Harris [Rochdale Hornets], Terry Cook [Halifax]; Dickie Williams [Leeds], Billy Banks [Huddersfield]; Mick Condon [Halifax], Tommy Harris [Hull FC], Elwyn Gwyther [Leeds], George Parsons [St Helens], Charlie Winslade [Oldham] and Glanville James [Hunslet]. The Other Nationalities, with three Warrington players appearing on their own ground, were represented by: Joe Phillips [Bradford Northern]; Brian Bevan [Warrington], Trevor Allan [Leigh], Pat Devery [Huddersfield], Lionel Cooper [Huddersfield]; Cec Mountford [Warrington], Neville Black [Keighley]; John Daly [Feathertstone Rovers], Wally Ellean [Rochdale Hornets], John Mudge [Workington Town], Harry Bath [Warrington], Arthur Clues [Leeds] and Dave Valentine [Huddersfield]. The referee was the excellent Mr A. Hill of Dewsbury.

Despite the slippery conditions both sides threw the ball about in good style. The overseas stars scored first with a great Lionel Cooper burst and exciting run to score a try wide out. Then Arthur chipped over, re-gathered and ran on to carry the brave Jack Evans the final five yards with him as he plunged over, Harry Bath converting. Next, Neville Black scooted over directly from a scrum and Bath converted before Wales hit back in style with Les Williams showing determination to score a good try. Jack Evans booted two goals to give a half time score of 13–7 to Other Nationalities. Dave Valentine took his team further ahead when he supported a Clues-Bath midfield move that had Bath clear through to Evans. He sent the terrific Valentine in for a 16–7 lead. Brave Wales hit back like champions with tries by Norman Harris and a powerful try from big George Parsons. At 16–13 it looked as though the overseas stars were going to lift the trophy with a win but that great hooker Tommy Harris had other ideas as he twisted and turned from dummy half, forced his way past a surprised Joe Phillips and dived in by the posts. Evans converted and Wales won the nail biter in the dying seconds 18–16.

With three teams: Wales, England and Other Nationalities on four points each from three games, it was the points difference that won the trophy for Other Nationalities as they finished with plus 24, Wales with minus 3 and England with minus 6. So Arthur received a winner's gold medal to go with his Yorkshire league winner's medal in 1947.

9

THE THIN END
OF THE WEDGE

In the days before Super League and annual contracts, a player was only allowed one fee when becoming a professional rugby league player. The only time a player was allowed another payment, other than match terms, was when a player was granted a benefit season or game for 10 years unbroken service to one club. The original payment was deemed as paid for 'relinquishing one's amateur status', therefore no further payment was allowed from any other club even if transferred to that club. There were of course illegal payments made to players by the buying club and these payments went under the devious title of 'back handers'.

Arthur was going into his sixth season for Leeds and, as time had gone by and he had learned the ways of British rugby league, he began to toy with the idea of asking the Leeds board for a new contract which would see out his entire playing career at Headingley. The original £750 he received for signing for the club had become a little outdated compared to the money being paid to players signing in the 1953–1954 season. He broached the subject with one or two of the club's directors and they said it would have to be discussed at board level. Arthur asked them to discuss this and let him know the outcome.

Bob McMaster had returned home in the summer of 1953 and one of the Leeds club's finest servants was about to play his last game of the season when Leeds opened their league account with a tough game against Hull FC at the Boulevard. Bert Cook, kicker of hundreds of goals for Leeds and a winner of many matches for the club with his wonderful place kicking and long distance punting of the ball played his last game for the club in this 23–14 defeat. He kicked one goal in the game and never played again in blue and amber. Bert went as player-coach to the grand club, Keighley. Two new players who had joined Leeds were local lad, Jack Lendill, a promising utility back who was brought up on the Hawksworth estate in Leeds, near to Kirkstall Abbey, and that master footballer, former Wigan and England loose forward, Billy Blan. Arthur continued as captain of the Leeds team which had lost Arthur Staniland, Ken Ward, Harold Oddy and Johnny Feather (all had transferred to other clubs).

The second match of the new season saw quite a few changes from the team beaten at the Boulevard as Leeds opened their home account. The side involved in the 45–10 win over Doncaster was: Jones; Turnbull, Moore, Brown, Verrenkamp; Dickie Williams, Stevenson; Shillitoe, Wood, Gwyther, Arthur Clues, Poole and Blan. Arthur produced a captain's knock in this game with a towering performance complete with one of his hallmark tries. A trip to the Watersheddings at Oldham was next for Arthur and his team to take on a side quickly developing into a formidable force in the league. Oldham won the tough battle 14–5. Next, Leeds beat Bramley 31–8 at the Barley Mow as Leeds prepared for another Yorkshire Cup campaign with a hard first round tie with those redoubtable cup fighters, Featherstone Rovers.

The first leg of the County Cup was at Post Office Road and Leeds came away with a surprising 21–7 success. The following week, Leeds used the wide open spaces of the Headingley ground to run the brave Rovers around in a 32–7 win, giving an aggregate score of 53–14 to Leeds. Again Arthur was the outstanding forward in both County Cup wins. He registered another superb try in the second leg. The first round win earned Leeds the plum tie of round two with a trip to Odsal and possibly another chapter of the Clues v Traill saga.

Drew Turnbull had started where he left off as his season began with 18 tries in the first 10 games. The player was in truly international form as most of his tries were splendid efforts. Warrington (at home beaten 43–14) and Leigh (at Hilton Park beaten 28–18) were duly dispatched into the win-bin. But going to Odsal in excellent spirits aiming to progress in the Yorkshire Cup, Leeds were unexpectedly beaten easily by 27–9 and again the running battle ensued between Arthur and Ken Traill with the big Aussie winning the physical battle, if not the game, by a wide points margin. York were beaten at Clarence Street 9–7 on 3rd October, the best of a disastrous month of results for Leeds. But it was back to representative football for Arthur as on 7th October 1953 when he was once again chosen to play for the Other Nationalities against Wales at Odsal in the European International Championship.

Wales, the runners up the previous season, were in determined mood, fully motivated to recapture the European crown and they selected a big, strong side to get their representative season off to a good start. As usual the Welsh backs were clever footballers and their pack contained four big men in Thorley, Hopper, Parsons and Tierney. The full side was: Jack Evans [Hunslet]; Steve Llewellyn [St Helens], Les Williams [Hunslet], Don Gullick [St Helens], Arthur Daniels [Halifax]; Dickie Williams [Leeds], Billy Banks [Huddersfield]; John Thorley [Halifax], Tommy Harris [Hull FC], Bill Hopper [Leeds], George Parsons [St Helens], Mal Tierney [Belle Vue Rangers] and Bryn Goldswain [Oldham]. The Other Nationalities selected their usual strong, fast, brilliant three-quarters and their world class pack and had the wonderful Phillips at full back and a new combination at half back. The team was: Joe Phillips [Bradford Northern]; Brian Bevan [Warrington], Tony Paskins [Workington Town], Pat

Devery [Huddersfield], Lionel Cooper [Huddersfield]; Johnny Robinson [York], Neville Black [Keighley]; Bevan Wilson [Workington Town], Wally Ellean [Rochdale Hornets], John Mudge [Workington Town], Harry Bath [Warrington], Arthur Clues [Leeds] and Dave Valentine [Huddersfield]. Almost 15,000 spectators turned out and the referee was the great Mr Charlie Appleton of Warrington.

Since the reintroduction of this competition the four games between Wales and the Other Nationalities had, by and large, been entertaining and as skilful as one would imagine with so many talented footballers on view. This fifth game was no less skilful or entertaining but the score line was vastly different to the previous close results with a massive 30–5 win for the Other Nationalities team. Playing brilliant rugby the Other Nationalities top quality backs ran the Welsh ragged with Lionel Cooper at his belligerent best crashing over for a superb hat trick of tries. 'Bev' chipped in with one of his memorable long range tries and Pat Devery, using Lionel Cooper as foil, scored a footballers' try. Wally Ellean kidded his way over from close in. Joe Phillips kicked four goals and Devery two. For a rather sorry Wales, Dickie Williams scored a neat try and Jack Evans kicked a goal. Robinson and Black had outstanding games, playing behind a pack that worked hard, then took complete control with the deadly duo of Clues and Bath running riot in midfield. This combination of two brilliant Australian forwards was a joy to watch. The supporters of both Warrington and Leeds accepted that they watched something very special each week. The 'Old Fox' Harry Bath headed back to Aussie club football at the back end of a wonderful career after making himself a legend in Sydney. The eternal sorrow is that the Australians never saw Arthur Clues at his consistently brilliant best. Had Arthur decided to go back home and have two or three seasons in Sydney, he would have achieved a reputation second to none. The 22 year old youth who wowed the Aussie supporters in the 1946 Lions tour tests had matured into the great all round forward.

So the overseas boys achieved their first goal, a win against Wales. Eleven days later came yet another legendary meeting, and a definite entry into the biff, bang, wallop history books. It was the third and final clash of the two antagonists Arthur and Edouard, Clues v Ponsinet. Arthur missed the Halifax game at Headingley the week after the Wales game with a thigh strain. Halifax won the game 40–10. He also missed the Hunslet game at Parkside the week after as he was in France with the Other Nationalities. They played this tough encounter at Stade Municipal, Bordeaux, on 18th October 1953. The referee was the very experienced Mr Charlie Appleton of Warrington, chosen, no doubt because of his ability to deal with the potentially explosive encounter. The French fancied their chances at home, as they always do, and selected the boxing policeman, Ponsinet, simply to frighten Arthur. This of course did not happen because where Arthur was concerned words like red rag and bull spring to mind. The teams lined up as follows, France: Puig-Aubert; M. Voron, C. Teisseire, A. Carrere, R. Contrastin; J. Merquey, J. Crespo; A. Carrere, J. Audoubert, F. Rinaldi, R. Bernard, E. Ponsinet and R. Guilhem. The team contained a big, rough, tough pack with pace in the backs and a match winning goal kicker in Puig-Aubert. The Other Nationalities selected a familiar looking team but Tommy Lynch came into the centre for the injured Pat Devery and the big Aussie back rower, Rex Mossop of Leigh partnered Arthur in the second row as Harry Bath was out injured. The team was: Joe Phillips [Bradford Northern]; Brian Bevan [Warrington], Tony Paskins [Workington Town], Tommy Lynch [Halifax], Lionel Cooper [Huddersfield]; Johnny Robinson [York], Neville Black [Keighley]; Bevan Wilson [Workington Town], Wally Ellean [Rochdale Hornets], John Mudge [Workington Town], Rex Mossop [Leigh], Arthur Clues [Leeds] and Dave

Valentine [Huddersfield].

Arthur had devised a game plan for his attack on big Edouard. Simply give him the ball and Arthur would clean him out! But how to give him the ball at the right time and in the right place was the problem. Arthur talked it over with Neville Black and when Arthur said, 'Go,' Neville, a good kicker of the ball, would put up a bomb to Ponsinet and Arthur would arrive at the same time as the bomb! It was a simple and effective ploy. Seizing the moment in the match, Arthur called 'Go!' and Neville obliged. Up went the ball and after it raced Arthur, straight at Ponsinet. No matter how tough a player is, there is always a moment in rugby when they wish they were somewhere else. This was one of those moments for big Edouard. He saw Arthur running at him like an express train and realised he was going to come off worst in this encounter. There was no hiding place on the field, so he about turned and raced onto the running track that surrounded the playing field. He was off like Seb Coe with Arthur chasing like Steve Ovett. The French gendarmerie let Edouard run past them into the safety of the dressing rooms but stopped big Arthur from entering the Frenchman's sanctuary. As Robert Gate said in his superb obituary to Arthur in later years, 'Arthur always joked that by the time they returned to the field of play, Brian Bevan had scored two beautiful tries and the game was won.' And win the Other Nationalities did 15–10. Johnny Robinson, the terrific stand off from York, scored the other try and Joe Phillips kicked three goals. For the French, their wingmen, Voron and Contrastin scored good tries and Puig-Aubert landed two goals. So the battle was won for Arthur. He wanted to fight but the boxer, big Ponsinet, would not! Arthur said that Ponsinet always sent him a Christmas card after that and maybe it's true as those days were very different from today.

Whilst Arthur chased the Frenchman, the grand referee, Mr Appleton, was reported to have said as Arthur disappeared from sight, 'We may as well continue because if he catches him it will be over quickly.' So the Other Nationalities got off to a flier in the European Championship with only England to beat to retain the Jean Galia trophy.

Arthur returned to his club side which lost to the strong Hunslet team at Parkside 8–7 whilst he had been in France. Arthur's first match back was Leigh at Headingley and this so called winning home banker ended in a disastrous 20–12 defeat. The final game that horrible October was the stiff away contest at Warrington. Packed with top players the Wire were well nigh invincible at fortress Wilderspool. Despite playing well Leeds lost the game 15–9.

Showing a remarkable change in form once October ended, Leeds went from 7th November until the final game of December 1953 losing only one game (on 28th November away to Halifax). The first game of that run was against Hull Kingston Rovers at Headingley, when Arthur led from the front and scored a beautiful try in the 56–5 demolition of the Robins. Lewis Jones scored a try and kicked 10 goals along with another Drew Turnbull hat trick of tries. Wakefield Trinity was seen off at Belle Vue by the huge score of 46–5, Jones kicking another eight goals with Gordon Brown and Ted Verrenkamp each registering a hat trick of tries. Arthur was in top form against Castleford in the next game when Leeds continued their revival with a stunning 48–14 win, George Broughton dashing over for three tries and Lewis Jones adding another nine goals. Next came the aforementioned Halifax defeat of 18–13 on 28th November. It coincided with Arthur missing the game as he played for the Other Nationalities.

With England having already beaten Wales and France, this game would decide the Champions of Europe for this season. The game was played at Wigan's Central Park and, for the first time in many years, not a Wigan player was in the England side. England selected: Ted Cahill [Rochdale

Hornets]; Peter Norburn [Swinton], Dougie Greenall [St Helens], Eppie Gibson [Workington Town], Frank Castle [Barrow]; Willie Horne [Barrow], Stan Kielty [Halifax]; Alan Prescott [St Helens], Harry Bradshaw [Dewsbury], Jack Wilkinson [Halifax], Charlie Pawsey [Leigh], Basil Watts [York] and Ken Traill [Bradford Northern]. It was a strong side indeed. The Other Nationalities went for the tried and tested players who had toughed it out in France earlier in the month with the exception of Tommy Lynch who made way for the fit Pat Devery in the centre and Neville Black was out injured at scrum half. His crucial role was filled by 'Fizzer' Dawson. Still missing was the great Harry Bath, out with a sore knee. The full overseas side was: Joe Phillips [Bradford Northern]; Brian Bevan [Warrington], Tony Paskins [Workington Town], Pat Devery, [Huddersfield], Lionel Cooper [Huddersfield]; Johnny Robinson [York], 'Fizzer' Dawson [Workington Town]; Bevan Wilson [Workington Town], Wally Ellean [Rochdale Hornets], John Mudge [Workington Town], Rex Mossop [Leigh], Arthur Clues [Leeds] and Dave Valentine [Huddersfield]. The referee was the strict Mr George Phillips [Widnes] and a healthy crowd of almost 20,000 enjoyed another fine exhibition of fast open football.

The England side played well above their normal European Championship level and with Bradshaw winning around 70 per cent of the ball from the set scrums the overseas side were chasing and tackling for much of the game. When they did gain possession the dangerous Bevan and Cooper were given plenty of ball. Bevan raced in twice for two memorable scores and Cooper again tore over from 30 yards for his one try. Johnny Robinson showed his evasive qualities once more and his strong burst brought him a grand stand off half's try. Phillips landed five goals. England's elusive full back, Ted Cahill, who would tour in the 1954 Lions side, scored a beautiful try and Eppie Gibson the big Workington Town schoolmaster produced a polished try too. Ken Traill, when not battling with Arthur, showed his classy ball handling and eye for an opening by scooting through for an opportunist's try and Frank Castle burnt the grass with his fantastic pace to score a beauty. Willie Horne kicked three goals for England but the outstanding display was from Peter Norburn the Swinton wingman or second row forward that was on debut at international level. He scored four cracking tries, earned rave reviews but never played for England again, one of the mysteries of the game at that time! The final result of 30–22 gave England the Championship and left a very disappointed overseas side wondering how they lost it.

There were two games for Leeds to play before the Christmas fixtures began. First was Keighley away, which gave them a 21–12 win. Next was Huddersfield at Headingley, which again ended in a fine win for Leeds 15–9. The Christmas Day game was at Mount Pleasant where Batley were beaten by Leeds 25–2. Boxing Day saw Wakefield Trinity at Headingley. The side were beaten 33–14. Batley came to Leeds on 28th December and Leeds ran up a 44–5 win.

This season the number of tries Arthur scored was below his high standard. He scored six tries all season, but these six were of the highest quality and were indeed memorable ones. In the win against Batley, he scored a fast second rower's try, tearing onto a midfield pass by Cliff Last, he stepped the full back and raced 35 yards under the posts.

The New Years Day game was at Fartown and started a four game run of defeats. Huddersfield won at Fartown 34–0 in a dreadful result for Leeds. This was followed by a loss to Doncaster away, by 19–8. Worse was to come as Hull FC outplayed Leeds at Headingley notching up 19–4. The old enemy, Bradford Northern, won at Odsal 9–4. Arthur missed the Huddersfield and Bradford Northern games because of injury and suspension. He returned at open side prop in the win over Dewsbury at Headingley 29–5. This game also saw the return of an old favourite, T.L. Williams at full back. Les had been looking after the 'A' team as player-coach and came in because of the retirement of Ralph Morgan and injury to Jimmy Dunn.

The up and down form of Leeds in the immediate weeks before the Challenge Cup competition started did not fill the team's supporters with confidence. All teams benefit from good league form as the cup comes around and Leeds had failed to hit any sort of form. The first round, first leg, was at Mount Pleasant, Batley, a ground on which Leeds had always found hard going and a difficult place to win. The first leg reflected this with Batley beating Leeds 20–13. Arthur was on top form with an outstanding display in defence and scoring a spectacular try up the slope. He was operating once again at open side prop, a position he did not prefer in normal circumstances, but with the youngster Shillitoe who played well at number eight injured, Arthur stepped up to control the scrum as pivot. Leeds suffered badly in this game as Billy Blan was stretchered off with a thigh injury and Tom Shirtliffe collapsed during the game and was advised to retire because of health problems. The injuries meant that Leeds finished the game with 11 men on the field.

The weather was terrible the following week with snow and ice threatening the return game. But when Saturday came, the game was on. Batley came to Headingley in the second leg and fell to the pace of the wing ace Drew Turnbull who scored a fabulous hat trick of tries. Leeds won 23–6 and went through to round two on an aggregate 36–26 win. Dewsbury were beaten 8–5 at Crown Flatt. On 5th March the tough Leigh came to Leeds in the second round of the cup. In an absolute thriller Leeds won through 12–3, with Lewis Jones and Cliff Last scoring tries and Jones kicking three goals. Two weeks later Leeds played Workington Town at Headingley in the crucial third round cup tie. All the time Arthur hoped that this could be the year he led out the Leeds team at Wembley and hopefully make up for the disappointment of the 1947 final. Workington had done wonders since joining the league in the late 1940s and had already appeared at Wembley in 1952 when they beat Featherstone Rovers 18–10. Indeed Workington went on to figure in two further Challenge Cup finals in 1955 against the winners Barrow, and again in 1958 when Wigan were the victors. As well as being recent cup winners Workington had also won the Championship in 1951 so the almost newcomers came to Headingley with a side brim full of fast, exciting players.

A crowd of 31,000 people were inside Headingley as the teams came out. Leeds, playing in the unusual colour of green jerseys had to be at their best against this confident Cumbrian outfit. Taking the ball from the very first scrum, Workington attacked through Harry Archer (the strong stand off half). Cec Thompson supported him and handed onto 'Fizzer' Dawson the Aussie scrum half who found the most underrated loose forward in the league, Billy Iveson, tearing onto the pass. Holding off Jimmy Dunn he crossed near the corner flag. Leeds were 3–0 down. With the Workington team playing with fire in their bellies, Leeds found it tough going. Gus Risman, the Workington player-coach, who was 43 years old the day after this game, brought off a superb tackle on Lewis Jones as the 'Golden Boy' tested the senior player's pace. Suddenly the score became 5–3 for Leeds as Jeff Stevenson opened up the Workington defence with a couple of outrageous dummies and had Drew Turnbull, dubbed the 'Flying Scotsman', scorching over in the corner. Jones added the perfect touch line conversion. Then Archer was semi concussed in a tackle from Arthur that forced the Cumbrians to switch Ike Southward from wing to stand off and carry the dazed Archer on the wing. On top now, Arthur introduced his famous side step to beat several tacklers in a mighty charge for the line and took three men over to score a typical Clues' try. Almost immediately Leeds attacked in their classic mode with Arthur setting loose Drew Turnbull with a tremendous long pass which found the rapid wingman in space. Up the touch line he sprinted, veering infield to Risman who, despite his vast experience, hesitated for a split second. That was all Turnbull needed and he swerved out again to the touch line to round the famous full back and sprint for the line to score a stupendous 70 yard try, Jones adding the goal. The final try of the half was a team affair as Stevenson, Clues, Alan Horsfall and Keith McLellan supported and handled superbly before Lewis Jones took the last pass and glided over. Leeds turned around 16–3 up and looked set for another semi final place.

With no substitutes in those days, the injured Archer continued on the wing with Ike Southward at stand off. Iveson almost had John Mudge over then Tony Paskins shot clear only to be tackled by Arthur, doing the basic job of second rower covering. Eppie Gibson drove through a gap and his explosive pace took him to the line for a fine try, converted by Risman. Lewis Jones broke beautifully from Arthur's wide pass and after a run of 40 yards drew Risman and sent Broughton charging over under the sticks, Jones goaling. Then Southward flashed over in the corner to make it 21–11 and the great Jeff Stevenson finished off Workington making a try for Cliff Last and scooting over himself. Both these tries were converted by Jones giving Leeds a 31–11 victory. The team could progress to the semi-final at Swinton to play the dreaded Warrington. Workington had made Leeds fight all the way but the injury to Harry Archer had disrupted their set plays. The teams on duty were, Leeds: Dunn; Turnbull, McLellan, Jones, Broughton; Brown, Stevenson; Horsfall, Wood, Hopper, Clues, Poole and Last. Workington had: Risman; Southward, Paskins, Gibson, Ivill; Archer, Dawson; Henderson, Lymer, Key, Mudge, Thompson and Iveson.

Leeds defeated York in the league at Headingley 23–10 with Arthur scoring another great try and also playing again at loose forward. Soon 3rd April rolled around and Leeds travelled to Station Road, Swinton, intending to break Warrington's hold on them in the Challenge Cup. Missing through injury was the excellent centre Keith McLellan. Broughton moved into the centre and Ted Verrenkamp came on to the wing. Despite a very tough and uncompromising game played in the true cup tie spirit before a gate of 37,000 and with some devastating tackling, especially by Arthur and Bernard Poole, Warrington maintained their 'evil eye' over Leeds. With tries by Jim Challinor and Brian Bevan and a goal by Harry Bath they claimed a deserved 8–4 win to take them to the twin towers. The Warrington side was: Frodsham; Bevan, Challinor, Stevens, McCormick; Price, Helme; Naughton, Wright, Lowe, Bath, Heathwood and Ryan. Warrington went on to play Halifax at Wembley on 24th April and drew 4–4 before 81,841 spectators. The replay at Odsal on Wednesday 5th May drew a world record attendance at a rugby league game when 102,569 people crammed into Odsal to see Warrington win the cup 8–4.

Of the six league games left, Arthur missed three. A long cup run, captain of the club, calls on Other Nationalities duty and his sports outfitters business had knocked him back a little. He still played in three of the last six games. Another issue irritating him was that the board couldn't agree whether or not to offer him another contract deal. They continued to put him off and this played on his mind.

Following the semi final defeat, Leeds struggled to beat Hull Kingston Rovers. But a score line of 18–17 gave the Loiners the win. Then on Good Friday, Hunslet destroyed Leeds at Headingley by 31–9 and the day after, Featherstone Rovers handed out another hard lesson by beating Leeds at Post Office Road 23–5. Easter Monday saw Castleford beaten away by 22–13 and the day after, Bramley were beaten 24–13 at Leeds. The final match of the season against Featherstone Rovers brought Leeds a humiliating defeat at Headingley 20–12.

10

FROM BLUE AND AMBER TO MYRTLE, FLAME AND WHITE

Arthur had the most disturbing close season since his arrival at Leeds in 1947. He considered that his request was not unreasonable when he asked the Leeds board to offer him another contract. It would be eight years at the end of the current season since he signed for the club but the directors seemed reticent about his request. Arthur had long maintained a friendship with the Hunslet Chairman, Mr Hector Rawson, and he asked his opinion as to what would be the correct way of approaching the Leeds board. Mr Rawson knew a way to remedy the situation immediately. He made an offer to Leeds for the transfer of the big Aussie from Headingley to Parkside. Hunslet would see that Arthur was satisfied about money and everyone concerned waited with bated breath for the Leeds board's reply. There was obvious concern amongst the Headingley board as Arthur was a living legend at the club and should it be seen that they wanted rid of their most famous commodity, there could be serious repercussions at the club amongst the supporters. So things were kept under wraps for the time being as it was the close season. Arthur wanted things sorted out as quickly as possible. From his point of view, either staying at Leeds or moving to Hunslet would suit his business requirements as his successful sports shop was in the city. It could have been awkward had any other club caught wind of Arthur's availability. A transfer into Lancashire for example would cause him business problems. All he could do was wait.

The season started for Leeds with a daunting trip up to the north west to tackle the tough Barrow at Craven Park. Arthur missed this game because of a thigh strain. He was back the following Tuesday for the trip to Rochdale Hornets and the result was a disappointing one as Leeds were beaten by the Hornets 13–7. Things were moving on the Hunslet front and the next game for Leeds was a home fixture against Dewsbury which, sadly, was Arthur's final game in the blue and amber of his beloved club. Arthur played at open side prop in this 34–16 win and the last Leeds team he played in was: Dunn; Scholes, McLellan, Wilkinson, Parker; Brown, Stevenson; Clues, Wood, Hopper, Sewell, Blan and Last.

On 28th August 1954 an era ended. Without doubt Leeds would struggle to find a more consistent international class second row forward than big Arthur. He had become, in a very short time, the centre point of the club. Everybody knew him and liked him. His character was gigantic and his influence on the team immense. Every club wanted him in their side. His playing ability could not be matched, here or in Australia. His skills were brilliant. He was the toughest of the tough, the hardest in a game brim full of hard men. He would leave a hole not only as a great player but as a man within the Headingley club. Now he was gone and folk wondered what the club would do without his guidance, charisma and toughness. His skill and team leadership would also be missed. From his debut for Leeds on 1st February 1947 to his final game on 28th August 1954, Arthur played 238 games for Leeds and scored 74 tries. No one like him would ever be seen again at Headingley.

The *Yorkshire Evening Post* sport page blazed the headline, 'Clues signs for Hunslet.' Now should the reader not know about the fierce rivalry between the Leeds and Hunslet clubs, may I just explain the depth of anguish felt by the Leeds supporters when this tragic news broke. Arthur Clues could have signed with any club in the league and that would have been bad enough, but to sign for Hunslet, well it was unacceptable and tantamount to swearing in church or in front of somebody's mum! It was just not done for a Leeds star, in his prime, to play for Hunslet. This was because the supporters of Hunslet (only a few minutes from Leeds town centre), detested the Headingley team with a passion!

Soccer supporters today talk of hating some club or other, well Hunslet and Leeds were the same. I have known grown men that loved rugby league and supported Leeds who would not go to the old Parkside ground just because Hunslet played there, even when Leeds were Hunslet's opponents. Leeds somehow felt superior to their near neighbours across the River Aire. Headingley was palatial in its splendid setting with the international test cricket ground and its big, wide immaculately kept rugby league ground on which test matches were played and huge crowds attended. Leeds were always in the market for overseas stars and even in those days were known as the 'Arsenal of Rugby League' because of their ability to import players from Australia and New Zealand and their willingness to spend money on the top players from rugby union. The Hunslet faithful could never come to terms with the Leeds club's wealth and this riled them which in turn got the backs up of the Leeds supporters. Hence there was no love lost between the two. Arthur had joined the enemy.

Hunslet did have its assets, including a stadium full of character which seemed to generate a charged atmosphere on match day. The club also produced some cracking home-grown players who came up through the wonderful Hunslet Schools Rugby League system. And probably because it had so many local players, the team seemed always to play with a never-say-die attitude.

Hunslet paid the transfer fee of £1,850 to Leeds and Arthur joined a healthy, close knit club still within easy reach of home and his business in the city. He signed for Hunslet at 30 years of age on 7th October 1954. In those days a forward had plenty left in the tank at age 30 and Arthur maintained a good turn of pace. His first game for Hunslet was at Parkside against Bradford Northern when he appeared with his old team mate, Dickie Williams, who had joined Hunslet in November 1953. Dickie had also captained the 1954 Lions tour to Australia and New Zealand. Two other Hunslet players, Alf Burnell and Geoff Gunney, had also toured under Dickie but had not yet returned when Arthur made his debut on 9th October.

With two key players missing, Hunslet looked a bit thin on the ground and in Arthur's first game, the team was: Eric Backhouse; Les Williams, Jimmy Bradshaw, Gordon Waite, Freddy Williamson; Dickie Williams, Arthur Talbot; Don Hatfield, Sam Smith, Brian Shaw, Ted Carroll, Arthur Clues and Glanville James. A big Hunslet crowd welcomed Arthur in the true tradition of rugby league people and Arthur didn't let them down. His debut for Hunslet was outstanding and not only did he score a spectacular try, he also brought the best out of big Don Hatfield, Brian Shaw and Welshman, Glanville James. The biggest cheer though was when the Bradford forward, Greaves, broke clear away and looked as though he would score a long distance try. Arthur set off after the Bradford man and, after a long chase, brought off a marvellous tackle to save the try. The Hunslet crowd, 16,000 on the day, rose to him as one and a star was born at Parkside. Hunslet won this game 16–0 with Les Williams scoring two tries, Dickie Williams scoring one try to go with Arthur's try. Eric Backhouse kicked two goals.

Batley at Mount Pleasant was the following game which Hunslet won 20–2. The next two games were away against York, which they lost 13–12 and Keighley at home, which they lost again, 14–6. Arthur missed both matches but he returned with a vengeance in the next game with a great performance against Hull FC at the Boulevard. In this 16–7 win, Arthur led the Hunslet pack in great style, and what an excellent pack it was, Hatfield, Gerry Welsh, Shaw, Gunney, Clues and Carroll. A week later, Castleford were beaten 15–7 at Parkside as the Hunslet forwards really began to hit form.

Representative football arrived again as Arthur was selected for the Northern Rugby League team that played an Australasian (combined Aussie and Kiwi players) team at Odsal before a crowd of 17,049. The Australasian team was: C. Churchill [Australia]; C. Eastlake [New Zealand], A. Watson [Australia], R. McKay [New Zealand], I. Moir [Australia]; R. Banks [Australia], K. Holman [Australia]; R. Bull [Australia], K. Kearney [Australia], W. McLennan [New Zealand], P. Diversi [Australia], K. O'Shea [Australia] and A. Atkinson [New Zealand]. The Northern Rugby League side was: J. Phillips [Bradford Northern]; B. Bevan [Warrington], Tony Paskins [Workington Town], Tommy Lynch [Halifax], Lionel Cooper [Huddersfield]; P. Metcalfe [St Helens], G. Helme [Warrington]; A. Prescott [St Helens], A. Wood [Leeds], D. Robinson [Wakefield Trinity], A. Clues [Hunslet], H. Bath [Warrington] and D. Valentine [Huddersfield]. The referee was Mr Charlie Appleton of Warrington. The result was a good 25–13 win for Australasia with Watson scoring two tries and Banks, Kearney and O'Shea also scoring tries. McKay kicked five goals. For Northern Rugby League, Bevan scored two tries and Cooper crossed for a try and Bath kicked two goals. The great triangle of back row forwards, Clues, Bath and Valentine were at their best again and only the sterling work of Roy Bull, Ken Kearney, Peter Diversi and Kel O'Shea could come anywhere near matching the fabulous three. This game, played at the end of the World Cup series, showed an all round improvement in the Southern Hemisphere team's skills with

Keith Holman proving to be arguably the best half back in the world. The Australian players who went back home could only relate stories of just how good Clues and Bath had become since making the long trip from Australia.

Arthur returned to the Hunslet side for the game against Halifax at Thrum Hall which Hunslet lost 26–12. He also figured in the next six consecutive games, all won as Hunslet approached the Christmas period with confidence. The games were: York, at Parkside (13–3 to Hunslet); Batley at home (14–0 to Hunslet); Featherstone Rovers also at home (15–13 to Hunslet in a game in which Arthur scored a powerful try); then home again against Hull FC on Christmas Day (16–0 to Hunslet); Boxing Day at Crown Flatt (18–2 to Hunslet); and then Huddersfield on New Years Day at Parkside (20–10 to Hunslet). Arthur missed the following away game at Doncaster, which Hunslet lost 15–11.

The 22nd January 1955 was a special day for Arthur as it was the first time since his transfer that he would play against Leeds. This match was heavily attended and Parkside was full to the brim, so much was Arthur loved by Leeds and now Hunslet supporters. To say that Hunslet won the game 13–2, goes nowhere near describing the game Arthur played. He was outstanding in a fine Hunslet performance. Leeds were on a 10 match unbeaten run and were easily favourites to win this game. The teams were, Hunslet: Backhouse; Snowden, Evans, Waite, Williamson; Williams, Talbot; Hatfield, Smith, Shaw, Gunney, Clues and James. Leeds fielded: Dunn; Turnbull, McLellan, Jones, Scholes; Brown, Stevenson; Anderson, Skelton, Poole, Hopper and Last. Arthur had a hand in all three Hunslet tries by Waite, Snowden and Freddy Williamson as he produced a performance which turned the clock back and outshone any previous display for Hunslet. Legend has it that Arthur was chaired off the field after the game by the Leeds supporters who wanted him to know just how they still felt for him. The next games were Castleford away and Bramley at home. Hunslet beat both teams 21–16 and 19–9 respectively before Whitehaven came to Parkside in round one of the Challenge Cup. Hunslet had had an early exit from the Yorkshire Cup before Arthur had joined them so the Challenge Cup was of even more significance this season. Hunslet fancied their chances as the pack were going strongly and the backs were scoring regularly.

Although they were a strong team up in Cumbria, Whitehaven were less effective when playing away and the Parksiders won in great style, 43–10, with Arthur producing a Clues special and scoring a long range try. The Hunslet side were particularly strong in the half backs with Alf Burnell and Arthur Talbot battling for the scrum half spot and the current Great Britain captain, Dickie Williams and the highly promising Brian Gabbitas going for the number six jersey. This again had all the hallmarks of a great cup team, strong in the pack and halfs, with pace in the backs.

The tough Halifax came to Hunslet in the league game and won a real rough house match by 10–6. Arthur missed this game as he was serving a one match suspension. The tough Halifax pack steamrollered their way to a win thanks to their strong pack including, John Thorley, Alvin Ackerley, Jack Wilkinson, Albert Fearnley and Les Pearce. Back for the second round tie against Hull Kingston Rovers at Craven Park, Arthur was in good form but late in the game took a heavy knock in the ribs. The result of the cup tie was a resounding win for Hunslet by 33–2. Then it was over to Humberside for the crucial third round game against Hull FC at the Boulevard. Before the game at the Boulevard, Hunslet were beaten at Post Office Road 18–12 by the strong Featherstone Rovers.

The Boulevard was just about the worst place to get a result in a cup tie in those days. Their forwards were awesome. With an international front row of Mick Scott, Tommy Harris and Bob Coverdale and a back three of Bill Drake, Harry Markham and the peerless John Whiteley, Hull FC were a mighty team indeed. But Hunslet went that day with a determination and resolve that would not be shaken. In the toughest game seen for many a year, the Parksiders fought through to a fine 7–5 win. So Arthur, along with Dickie Williams, was on the verge of another Wembley appearance, the one thing he had coveted since that day back in 1947 when Leeds fell to Bradford Northern. He had played in five semi-finals with Leeds (including a draw) and won only one. This time he was with Hunslet and the side that stood in the way was the doughty cup fighters, Barrow. The game was played at Central Park, Wigan on 2nd April 1955 and as there was no local involvement the crowd was a disappointing 25,493.

The teams lined up, Hunslet: Talbot; Snowden, Evans, Waite, Williamson; Williams, Burnell; Hatfield, Smith, Shaw, Gunney, Clues and James. The Hunslet pack was second to none in the league. The half backs were fresh back from last summer's Lions tour and all seemed set for Arthur and Dickie Williams to forget the disappointments of those five failures and go through to the fabled twin towers once again. The Barrow side to beat was: Best; Lewthwaite, Jackson, Goodwin, Castle; Horne, Toohey; Belshaw, McKeating, Barton, Grundy, Parker and Healey. This was a tough, durable side. On the day the Barrow boys were too tough for Hunslet and went to Wembley for the second time in five years on the back of a 9–6 win. It was heartbreak again for Arthur. There was another disappointment the Friday after too as Hunslet travelled to Headingley only to loose 22–12. Arthur was again the best forward on the field and as if it had been arranged, at the end of the game Arthur was again chaired from the field by the Leeds supporters. Never have the feelings of a team's supporters shown through towards a player as they did for big Arthur in the first two games he played against Leeds after his transfer. The score book shows that the big man also scored Hunslet's first try in this game, just to remind the Leeds faithful of all his mighty deeds for the club. In the next game, Leigh won at Parkside 25–13. Arthur missed the following match at home to Dewsbury which Hunslet won 49–2. He was back for the 30–25 defeat at Odsal by Bradford Northern but missed the game at Keighley when Hunslet went down to a bad 19–7 defeat. Returning the week after, Wakefield Trinity pulled back a few recent defeats to beat Hunslet, 25–7. In the penultimate game of the season, against Hull KR at home, Hunslet gained a 44–11 win in which Arthur played with a broken finger yet had a good game. Arthur missed the final match of the season which was a win at the Barley Mow against Bramley 34–10.

If one takes into account the depressing disappointment of the semi-final defeat, it seems only human nature that a poor run of form would hit as it did after the Barrow cup tie with just three wins in eight games. In the 1954–1955 season, Arthur played in 23 out of a possible 31 games and scored four tries. His worth to the Hunslet team was in his undoubted leadership both on and off the field. He, as usual, never shirked in attack or defence and both the young and not so young at Parkside benefited from his arrival.

11

ENJOYING PARKSIDE

The 1955–1956 season was a traumatic one for Arthur. He played in the first six games in which Hunslet won five and lost one, he then missed two games because of an ankle injury picked up in the Other Nationalities v England game at Wigan. He returned for one match which Hunslet won, then received the sad news that his father had died at home in Parramatta. Arthur travelled back to Australia to settle his father's affairs and missed 11 games for Hunslet from 1st October to 26th December.

Hunslet started the season with a great win over Swinton at Parkside 25–16. Arthur was on the score sheet with a good try. Hunslet next had a hard fought win at Doncaster, 17–5. In the 23–10 win over Featherstone Rovers Arthur was back on the score sheet with a cracking try. Arthur then led the Hunslet pack to a resounding away win at the tough Watersheddings ground of the Oldham club by a score of 15–8. Castleford were beaten away 17–13 and the only game Hunslet lost in this period was against Bradford Northern at Odsal by 27–23 in the first round of the Yorkshire Cup. This was the game played between the wins against Doncaster, away and Featherstone Rovers at home. After this came the most convincing win of any game that Arthur played in for the great Other Nationalities side. This was against England in a newly organised European Championship. Wales had unfortunately dropped out of the competition because of the sudden lack of Welsh rugby union players changing codes thus leaving the principality sadly short of international class men. A lifeline was thrown to the great Welsh players already in the game by allowing their inclusion into the Other Nationalities team. Whilst it was sad to see the demise of the Welsh National side, it worked wonders for the already strong overseas outfit.

The Other Nationalities side that played England at Central Park, Wigan on 12th September 1955 was: Glyn Moses [St Helens]; Brian Bevan [Warrington], Tommy Lynch [Halifax], Lewis Jones [Leeds], Billy Boston [Wigan]; Ray Price [Warrington], Billy Banks [Huddersfield]; John Thorley [Halifax], Tom McKinney [Warrington], Bob Kelly [Wakefield Trinity], Harry Bath [Warrington], Arthur Clues [Hunslet] and Dave Valentine [Huddersfield]. The nationality count was six Welshmen, three Australians, two Irishmen, one New Zealander and one Scotsman. The England side read as follows: Jimmy Ledgard [Leigh]; Mick Sullivan [Huddersfield], Phil Jackson [Barrow], Dennis Goodwin [Barrow], Terry O'Grady [Oldham]; Joe Mullaney [Featherstone Rovers], Frank Pitchford [Oldham]; Alan Prescott [St Helens], Sam Smith [Hunslet], Jack Wilkinson [Halifax], Don Robinson [Wakefield Trinity], Reg Parker [Barrow] and Ken Traill [Bradford Northern]. The referee was the great Mr Ron Gelder of Wakefield and the gate for this Monday evening international game was a healthy 18,232.

In less than two minutes, Ken Traill and Arthur were toe to toe in their usual title fight. Ron Gelder read the riot act and, apart from the odd clout delivered when passing each other, things were quiet on the Clues-Traill front. The Other Nationalities were in sparkling form with the inseparable Bath, Clues and Valentine working in perfect rhythm. The classical work of Clues and Bath created breaks for the ever alert Valentine. The big Scot linked with Ray Price and Billy

Banks who provided both Tommy Lynch and Golden Boy Lewis Jones the space for an electric centre partnership that enthralled the big crowd. They in turn engineered running chances for the powerful Boston to romp in for a hat trick of tries and the 'Peter Pan' of wingmen, the brilliant Brian Bevan, scored two tries worth paying the admission money to see. At one point, Harry Bath followed a Clues charge at the line and accepted his second row partner's back flip pass to crash over for a try. A further try and six magnificent goals by Lewis Jones gave the Other Nationalities 33 points. England, although outplayed, did act out a major part in this superb rugby league contest and the centre pairing of the two huge Barrow middle backs, Jackson and Goodwin, helped Mick Sullivan to score a beautiful try and Don Robinson to use his bulk to crash through four tackles to register his touchdown. The ever reliable Jimmy Ledgard landed five good goals to give England a final score of 16.

This was a truly wonderful exhibition of fast open football, with a smattering of biff, bang, wallop. Sad to say the rugby league world would only see one further paring of the fabulous Clues-Bath partnership the following season but, strange as it seems, the magnificent pair only played together 11 times. The legendary twosome was so outstanding together that their partnership seemed to go on forever.

Arthur missed Hunslet's home match against Bradford Northern in the league, a win of 16–3 as well as the home defeat by Leeds, 23–7. On 24th September, when he played in the win over Doncaster at Parkside by 34–23, this was his last game before his return to Australia for his father's funeral. In Arthur's absence Hunslet's results were: Barrow away (Hunslet lost 31–2); Oldham home (Hunslet lost 26–11); Wakefield Trinity away (Hunslet lost 24–2); Leigh away, [BBC Floodlit Competition] (Hunslet lost 46–20); Swinton away (Hunslet lost 12–4); Barrow home (Hunslet lost 25–13);

Liverpool City away (Hunslet lost 33–13); Wakefield Trinity home (Hunslet lost 12–11); York away (Hunslet won 8–4); Keighley away (Hunslet lost 33–6); and Huddersfield home (Hunslet won 25–6). Of the 11 games played without Arthur, Hunslet lost nine and only won two.

Arthur returned for the Hull FC game at the Boulevard on 26th December which Hunslet lost 22–5. The following day the 'Airlie Birds' came to Parkside and won again, this time by the reduced margin of 14–5. Four days later a trip to Post Office Road was again without Christmas cheer as Hunslet were beaten 23–9 by Featherstone Rovers. On the first Saturday in 1956, Hunslet beat Batley at home, 21–5 but lost a week later at Fartown to Huddersfield, 8–7. Bradford Northern beat them at Odsal 18–3 but Hunslet put the wheels back on with a win over Hull KR at home, 17–7 and another win at home against Keighley, 11–8, put them in confident mood to take on Bradford Northern at Parkside in the first round of the Challenge Cup.

Having beaten Northern earlier in the season at Parkside, Hunslet fancied their chances but fell 10–9 in a bitter defeat. The Hunslet board of directors had received a tip off about a young forward playing for the amateur club Lock Lane in Castleford. He was just out of the army after completing his National Service and had spent some time abroad, coming back to Castleford looking tanned and fit. The board members went to see the lad at his home and invited him down to Parkside to train with the first team with a view to signing on for the club. Having been away for a couple of years and being a player, not a watcher of the game, he hardly knew anything about Arthur. But after training with Arthur for about an hour, the youngster headed over to where the board were all watching his progress and said, 'I will sign now if you want.' The board were delighted, took him into the boardroom and signed him. When asked what persuaded him to sign he said, 'Training with Arthur Clues. He has shown me more in that hour than I learned in all my time in amateur football.'

When asked what Arthur had shown him, he said that when playing at loose forward Arthur had taught him to always come out of the set scrum with his both elbows bent level with his shoulders. As Arthur told him, 'If you do that son, you will hit one of the opposing forwards coming around to get your scrum half.' The lad's name was Harry Poole!

Hunslet lost to Bramley across at the Barley Mow by 12–5 on the day that Harry Poole made his debut but beat Batley at Mount Pleasant 19–12. Then Hunslet beat Hull KR at home 36–16. The following week Hull Kingston Rovers gained sweet revenge with a good 16–14 win when Hunslet paid a visit to Craven Park. Then Leeds had a big win against the old enemy at Headingley on Good Friday to the tune of 35–14. Arthur loved his return to Leeds despite the heavy defeat. He had played in 14 consecutive games since coming back from Australia. The Leeds game caught up with him when he damaged a calf late in the game. The day after, Hunslet beat Bramley at Parkside by 21–7 without Arthur and two days later, on Easter Monday, were beaten by Halifax at home 15–9.

For Hunslet it had been a long, hard season without Arthur for so many games but he never shirked his matches and came back with a bang despite losing in this game against the tough Halifax pack. In the final few games of the season he missed Castleford at home, a win of 18–15, but was back for the tough trip to Thrum Hall to once again play Halifax. In this game the Hunslet team suffered a rough encounter and received a severe 30–7 defeat. Arthur seemed to be targeted for particularly rough treatment being thumped from the start by the big Thrum Hall pack and finished the game battered and bruised. Arthur missed the final game of the season when Hunslet ran in 41–18 against Liverpool City a game in which Harry Poole kicked seven goals and Geoff Gunney scored five tries, a remarkable feat for both the young forwards.

So once again another season closed. This particular season was a sad one for Arthur and Muriel as the loss of Arthur's dad in Australia brought home to him just how far away he was from his family. His business was going well in Leeds and he was enjoying his rugby, even though it was not the most successful spell in his long career. Because of his 11 weeks spent in Australia, Arthur had a hit and miss season of appearances and managed only 23 games. He had also lost his knack of scoring tries, managing only two tries in 23 matches. On the positive side Hunslet had lots of good youngsters on their books and the experienced men were in the correct positions. Young Billy Langton was pushing to make the full back role his own, good kids such as Allan Preece, Denis Tate, Willie Walker, Jimmy Stockdale, Colin Sutcliffe, Frank Child and Jack Firn were making great progress. Brian Gabbitas was just about the best young stand off in the league. The old stagers who supported these young guns, Alf Burnell, Arthur Talbot and Gordon Waite, did a great job bringing on the kids. Alan Snowden, Tommy Potter and the soon to be signed South African, Ronnie Colin, gave the side plenty of pace and strength on the flanks. In the pack young Colin Cooper was learning the prop forward's job and the regular players now had a look of becoming a real force in the league. Possibly the strongest all round pack which Hunslet could select at the time would be Don Hatfield, a great ball winner in the scrum, Sam Smith an international hooker in his own right, Brian Shaw, who would go on to represent Great Britain in three positions, Arthur Clues, Geoff Gunney a big, fast international forward and Harry Poole who would captain a Lions touring side in 1966 and develop Hull Kingston Rovers into a great side later in his career. Welsh international, Glanville James, and utility player, Gordon Waite, made up the other top forwards in the squad. Arthur could see the club's potential.

12

THE END OF A PLAYING LEGEND

The Halifax side that had roughed up Arthur late in the previous season when they battered Hunslet at Thrum Hall, were playing this season in the Lancashire League as the top Yorkshire clubs of the previous season did, to even up the Yorkshire and Lancashire leagues. Last season Halifax had been successful and won the Yorkshire Cup and the Yorkshire League. They had fought through to Wembley in the Challenge Cup, only to loose to Saints. They had also lost out to Hull in the old top four Championship Trophy. Halifax had also signed Arthur's arch enemy, Ken Traill, from Bradford Northern. But what upset Arthur was that he could not take revenge for the hiding he took at Thrum Hall. This was because Hunslet had not had such a good league season, therefore the two clubs would not meet in the league this coming campaign. He would have to be patient and wait his time.

Hunslet (and Arthur) got off to a flying start against Wakefield Trinity at home in the first game of the season. Arthur scored a good try in the 16–14 win. Hunslet lost the following two games, which were Huddersfield at home (13–9 to Huddersfield) and Swinton away (13–7 to Swinton). Arthur played at blind side prop at Swinton in a pack that read, Colin Cooper, Sam Smith, Arthur, Harry Poole, Geoff Gunney and Glanville James.

Doncaster were swept out of the Yorkshire Cup at Parkside 45–0 and Batley were dispatched a week later

39–14, again at Parkside. Hunslet then beat Castleford at Wheldon Road in round two of the County Cup, 26–9 and the Hunslet players could smell a cup winning run at last. Leigh beat the best team Hunslet could field the following week as the Lancashire boys turned on the razzmatazz at Hilton Park to win 40–14. The big Aussie scored a beautiful try to no avail. Arthur missed the next game, a 29–11 win against Workington Town at home, with a niggling knee injury.

York at Clarence Street was the next vital game which was the semi-final of the Yorkshire Cup. With Denis Tate in at stand off for the injured Brian Gabbitas, Hunslet played just the right game, with Arthur leading their strongest pack of Hatfield, Smith, Shaw, Clues, Poole and Gunney. What a pack! Hunslet came away with a fine cup win against a very strong York side on their own pitch. The score of 13–6 took the team into the Yorkshire Cup Final to play Wakefield Trinity at Headingley. So there was still a chance of a winner's medal for Arthur at his third attempt in a County Cup Final (the previous chances were the game Leeds drew and their subsequent defeat in the replay against Wakefield Trinity in 1947–48).

The league continued with an away game at Doncaster to give Hunslet a big 34–0 win. Then an even better performance came as Hull FC visited Parkside and were beaten 32–3. But the long trip to Whitehaven ended in a 22–12 defeat with Arthur missing the trip.

Bolstered by the great wins against Doncaster and Hull FC and despite the defeat at Whitehaven, Hunslet next travelled across Leeds to take on Wakefield Trinity at Headingley in the big County Cup game where the gate of 30,942 proved to be the fifth highest attendance ever in the history of the Yorkshire Cup. The teams were, Wakefield Trinity: F. Mortimer; Smith, A. Mortimer, Bell, Cooper; Holliday, Rollin; Harrison, Bridges, Haigh, Kelly, Armstead and Chamberlain. Hunslet's team was: Langton; Child, Stockdill, Waite, Preece; Gabbitas, Talbot; Hatfield, Smith, Cooper, Shaw, Clues and Gunney. Again in a cup final, Wakefield Trinity proved too strong for

Hunslet and with Les Chamberlain easily the best man on the field, won by 23–5. Try scorers for Trinity were Smith (two tries), Cooper (two tries) and A. Mortimer (one try). F. Mortimer kicked four goals. Frank Child scored the Hunslet try and Arthur Talbot kicked a goal. This meant a runners up medal for Arthur, yet again. Exactly one week after the Yorkshire Cup Final, Hunslet went to Belle Vue and beat Trinity 21–17. This was a good but ironic win.

The 1956–1957 season saw the Australian Kangaroo tourists arrive to attempt to take back the Rugby League Ashes. Part of the itinerary for the tour was a game to build up the funds of the tourists against a Northern Rugby League XIII. The game was played at Hilton Park, the home of the Leigh club. It was played on Monday 29th October 1956 and a crowd of 7,811 turned out to see an entertaining and hard fought game between two strong sides. It was the final time Arthur and Harry Bath played together.

Australia selected a strong, almost full strength test side which was: Gordon Clifford [Newtown]; Dennis Flannery [Ipswich], Tom Payne [Toowoomba], Alex Watson [Brisbane Wests], Des McGovern [Toowoomba]; Bob Banks [Toowoomba], Cyril Connell [Rockhampton]; Roy Bull [Manly-Warringah], Ken Kearney [St George], Brian Davies [Brisbane Brothers], Norm Provan [St George], Tom Tyquin [South Brisbane] and Kel O'Shea [Western Suburbs]. O'Shea came from the same club, Wests, as Arthur. The Northern Rugby League XIII put out a strong side: Frank Mortimer [Wakefield Trinity]; Brian Bevan [Warrington], Lewis Jones [Leeds], Laurie Gilfedder [Warrington], Malcolm Davies [Bradford Northern]; Dave Bolton [Wigan], Frank Pitchford [Oldham]; Ken Jackson [Oldham], Jack Keith [Oldham], Brian Shaw [Hunslet], Harry Bath [Warrington], Arthur Clues [Hunslet] and Derek Turner [Oldham].

The side selected for the Northern Rugby League XIII showed the tremendous strength and depth which the selectors had at their disposal. Bevan, Jones, Clues and Bath speak for themselves but Ken Jackson, the outstanding Derek 'Rocky' Turner, Dave Bolton, Laurie Gilfedder, Frank Pitchford and Brian Shaw all went on to be full Great Britain players. The back three of the pack were particularly strong and fierce with Harry Bath and Arthur again revelling in this representative selection and Derek Turner placing his marker down for further selection at a higher level. The Australians too were a powerful side and the togetherness of a touring team pulled them through for a good 19–15 win. McGovern scored two tries and Tyquin scored one try with Clifford kicking five goals. For the League XIII, Bolton, Pitchford and Shaw scored tries and Lewis Jones landed three goals. The referee was the experienced Mr Norman Railton of Wigan.

Apart from being the final game for Arthur playing alongside Harry Bath, it was Arthur's final representative game of his career. He had discussed his retirement with the Hunslet board but had promised to see out this season to the end. Arthur and Brian Shaw returned to the Hunslet side for the game against Leeds at Parkside and both forwards had a great game in the 12–5 victory. A tough match at Odsal was next on the agenda and a great away win was recorded 18–7. Hunslet then took on and beat Hull Kingston Rovers at home by 27–9.

The touring Australians were the next visitors to Parkside on Wednesday 21st November and Arthur led from the front to produce a creditable result, albeit an Aussie win by 27–11. On Tuesday 24th November, Hunslet travelled to the walled City of York to beat the 'Wasps' at Clarence Street by 14–7.

As Christmas beckoned, Hunslet had five games before a dreaded long trip to Cumbria on New Years Day. Starting with Dewsbury at home, the team won 9–5 with a back three of Jack Hirst, Stan Dodds and Arthur at loose forward, then Hunslet beat Whitehaven and Bramley at Parkside, 30–21 and 23–14 respectively. A defeat at the Boulevard 12–3 followed and the final game of 1956 saw a 10–6 win over Castleford at home.

On New Years Day 1957, Hunslet travelled up to the cold north west to face Workington Town. They had a fantastic 23–10 win. Oldham proved too tough and beat Hunslet in a nail biter, 5–2, in a match with more fights on the pitch than blades of grass. Next was York at home, which Hunslet won 15–10, followed by a victory over Batley at Mount Pleasant, 30–4. Featherstone Rovers gave Hunslet a shock by beating them 11–9 at Post Office Road. As he'd been away on business, Arthur had missed four games: Workington Town, Oldham, York and Batley. He returned for the defeat at Featherstone but was instrumental in winning the next games against Keighley, away 12–4, Batley at home in the first round of the Challenge Cup, 14–7 and Castleford at Wheldon Road, 27–7.

The season was quickly coming to a close and the next game was a crucial second round cup tie, again up in the wilds of Cumbria at the tight little Recreation Ground, Whitehaven. Like many before them on that graveyard of cup tie dreams, Hunslet lost, 7–0. Spirits were revived the following week with a 19–12 win at Parkside against Bradford Northern, with Arthur showing tremendous strength in scoring a memorable solo try. But then another shock came against Bramley at the Barley Mow with a 9–8 defeat. Hunslet beat Hull Kingston Rovers at Craven Park 23–8. This win was followed inconsistently by a 13–8 defeat by Swinton at Parkside. A great win at Fartown saw a score of 20–8 against Huddersfield, then in the win at Parkside over Featherstone Rovers, Arthur scored what would be his last ever try as he again led in fine style to a 17–7 win. An injury in the Featherstone game caused him to miss the home wins against Leigh, 16–6 and Doncaster, 30–0 but knowing he was almost retired, wild horses couldn't have kept him out of the Leeds game at Headingley on Good Friday evening and the big crowd gave him a standing ovation as he ran out on to the pitch for the last time. Leeds won the game but it mattered not. The score was 28–13 but Arthur went out in style by having a very good game.

Only three games were left: Oldham at Parkside on Easter

Saturday which Hunslet lost 21–12, Arthur then missed the match against Keighley at Parkside which Hunslet also lost 14–12 as he wanted to play his final game on the last day of the season just as he had promised the Hunslet board. His swan song was against Dewsbury at Crown Flatt and another big crowd applauded him all the way to the centre spot to toss the coin. The final result was a Hunslet win of 30–7. This was an outstanding winning end to such a fantastic career. Arthur had played in 34 out of a possible 45 games in this final season and had scored five tries. He had kept his word to the Hunslet board and his only sorrow was that Hunslet hadn't played Halifax in his last season. He could then have gone out in style against Ken Traill and those big tough Halifax forwards who had roughed him up in that game at Thrum Hall.

The final words about Arthur's Hunslet career are Geoff Gunney's words. He played alongside Arthur in the Hunslet team possibly more times than anyone. Geoff remembers the first time he faced Arthur as a 17 year old youngster when he played in only his fourth game for Hunslet against Leeds. At a play the ball after a long break and run by Geoff, Bob McMaster accidentally kicked Geoff between the eyes and he battled on for the remainder of the game without complaining. Arthur made his way over at the final whistle and put his arm around him and said, 'Well played young 'un, you'll do for me,' Geoff said, 'He was the best ever for me. A great player, as hard as nails and as skilful as any back.'

When Geoff was playing at loose forward one day, a well known good scrum half was giving Geoff a hard time by using the blind side of the scrum. Arthur told Geoff to swap positions with him for one scrum. The scrum half tried the blind side again and Arthur smacked him. Geoff said the half back never tried it again! 'He would look after you on the field, he was a great mate. He had some run-ins with nearly all the hard men knocking about then but the bloke he always had a dab at was Ken Traill. Mind you Trailly always had a go back so that got it on. He helped you get through your game, he always had some advice to give and in most cases it worked, he was brilliant.'

When Geoff got married and Alf Burnell was his best man, Arthur bought Geoff all the floor tiles for his new house as a wedding present. On the other hand, although the vast majority of the great forwards played a rough game in those days, Arthur could be exceptionally ruthless during a game. One hooker in particular who never gave in at the scrum used to reach with his legs right into the opposing part of the scrum in an effort to win back the ball. Arthur told him to stop or he would be sorry but the hooker just continued doing it. Then as the scrum collapsed shortly after his warning, Arthur raked the hooker's two legs from top to bottom with his studs and the hooker was carried off never to return that afternoon. That of course was an industrial hazard for hookers, they really were sitting ducks. With both arms around their props they were wide open for a smack. Similarly they were vulnerable when reaching into their opponent's half of the scrum.

Keeping himself fit during the close season, Arthur started training with Hunslet, without playing, to ease down steadily. Hunslet's first three games were Doncaster at Parkside followed by York and St Helens away.

The following story came from the late Stan Moyser, the tough hooker-come-prop of the Halifax club. One Tuesday evening at Thrum Hall before Hunslet's fourth game of the season against Halifax, Stan walked into the dressing room to see most of the players reading the *Halifax Evening Courier* newspaper. According to Stan this was what happened: 'All the players were reading the back page and one or two were looking nervous. "Look at this Stan," Albert Fearnley said, and there as large as life in two inch headlines it said "Clues makes come back against Halifax".

'A lot of players said, "I never touched him in those matches." Whether they'd touched him or not, as the players exited the old wooden dressing shed there was Arthur as large as life waiting outside.

"Hi fellers, are yer ready for it?" Arthur asked ominously. And Arthur hit every one of the forwards from the kick off. He hit both centres and even the full back. But the player he hit most was Ken Traill. Arthur hit Traill every time he passed him.'

'The referee was Mr Tom Watkinson, a schoolteacher and a good referee. He knew that Arthur was playing for one thing, revenge. The referee would allow little things but not such all out violence. At half time the Hunslet secretary, Harry Jepson, always allowed his late wife Mary to take three cups of tea in for the officials. This time, as Mr Watkinson knew Harry was also a teacher, he asked Mary if she would ask Harry to have a word with Arthur in the dressing room and ask him to stop hitting Ken Traill. Harry Jepson knew Arthur's blood was up and said, "Don't talk silly Tom," or words to that effect when Mary passed on the message.'

Arthur gained all the revenge he wanted that afternoon and Hunslet won 16–12. Arthur just had one last request from the Hunslet board. That was to allow him to play at the Boulevard in the Yorkshire Cup the following week just to say farewell to those superb Hull FC fans. He did play and the club knowing that this was definitely his final game made him captain for the day. As there was a junior curtain raiser on the pitch, both junior teams waited on the wooden steps for the run onto the field from the dressing rooms of the senior sides. Harry Jepson stood next to Arthur as he waited to run onto the pitch. At the side of him was the late, great Mick Scott, the Hull FC captain. Arthur's final words as a player to one of his tough opponents was to look straight into Mick Scott's eyes and say, 'Well Scotty, do you want it easy or f****** hard this afternoon?'

Mick Scott knew the score and said with a smile, 'Easy will do Arthur and the best of luck to you.' Arthur had respect to the very end.

13

RETIREMENT AND LIFE AFTER FOOTBALL

After Arthur retired from the game he concentrated on his sports outfitters business. He had a gift of making friends and contacts which helped him as he was building up his shop. It became the best known of its type in the city. An example of his shrewd business brain and contacts was on the Australian Kangaroo tour of 1956, he spoke to the tour manager and offered the tourists three sets of playing kit for the price of two. Arthur explained to the Aussies that by accepting his offer they would save money on excess baggage. They agreed and Arthur made a good profit on the deal as well as earning a contact for deals with Australian tours. Everyone knew about Arthur's shop, from international cricket stars to professional rugby players to the bread and butter amateur soccer lads. All knew they would get a good deal at 'Cluesy's'.

It was thought that Arthur would make an ideal coach at the end of his playing days but somehow a full move into coaching never took off. He did coach the Australian 1960 World Cup team in a competition won by Great Britain who beat Australia 10–3 at Odsal. His coaching career at Leeds only lasted three weeks. Roy Francis agreed to join Leeds as coach and Arthur stood in as acting coach while Roy worked a three weeks' notice period at Hull FC. Arthur did eventually rejoin his beloved Leeds when he was invited to join the Leeds football committee to become actively involved in the recruitment of new players.

After a heart attack, Arthur decided to take his doctor's advice and sell his sports outfitters. He sold out in 1977 and after over 25 years of working hard in the business, he looked forward to a long and easy retirement. This never really happened as Arthur was something of a workaholic. He took up a position as a sales manager for the oil and fuel company, Charrington Hargreaves and continued to work for the football committee at Headingley. He then accepted an invitation to act as the Sports Minister's representative on the Yorkshire and Humberside Sports Council. His success as a top rugby league player and cricketer, as well as being a good golfer, combined with his wonderful ability to make friends, made him the ideal man to attend Sports Council meetings acting for the Minister and making sure that the public money was going to the correct places. 'I don't pull any punches,' he told The *Yorkshire Post's* feature writer John Thorpe some years ago in an article about his work, 'If anyone is trying to get easy money, I speak my mind. On the other hand, if any deserving cause applies for a grant and it is genuine, then I support that claim.' Arthur served five Sports Ministers as a watchdog which was a record at the time. He must have been good at his job.

Arthur and Muriel lived in a beautiful house in a leafy Leeds suburb. On display in the house were photographs of Arthur with sporting and political friends he made over his years as a great sportsman and a successful businessman. In pride of place was a photograph of Arthur posing with former Australian Prime Minister, Bob Hawke. There were also several photographs of Arthur with some of the world's greatest cricketers, including Keith Miller, Richie Benaud and many others. His great friend, the High Commissioner of Australia was also on display. The big Aussie from Parramatta often acted as host to famous sportsmen, film stars, politicians and businessmen who would call in to say hello.

Nothing or no one could change Arthur and nothing ever seemed to faze him. This is exemplified by the story he told John Thorpe in his interview. The occasion was a farewell dinner at the House of Lords for the retiring Australian High Commissioner who introduced Arthur to a fellow guest. Whilst being on his best behaviour, Arthur didn't know this bloke from Adam, but not wanting to let Doug, the High Commissioner down, he thought he had better make some small talk with him. 'Well mate, how do you make a crust then?' Arthur asked this very well dressed guest in true Aussie style.

The guest smiled and replied, 'Actually I own the Canadian Bank.'

Not put off for a second, Arthur said, 'Well that's not a bad line mate,' as Doug fell about laughing.

As Mr Thorpe said, only Arthur could have got away with a faux pas of that magnitude at a diplomatic function.

Arthur could master anything he put his mind to, this included the yo-yo. He could do anything with that toy, walk the dog, double loop, back flip, any exercise at all came easily to him. Drawn away to Workington Town in a cup tie, Leeds decided to make the trip by rail and hired a carriage for the trip. With so many empty seats available, the carriage was filled by supporters wanting to make the journey up to the north west. Arthur's duty that day was to act as a kind of courier and to help the trip on to a successful conclusion. To entertain the supporters, Arthur took along his yo-yo and before long had the travellers in stitches with his routines. The chairman of the supporters' club was a senior citizen who loved being in Arthur's company. Arthur performed a trick with the yo-yo that involved flicking out the toy and bringing it back to his hand. He could knock a cigarette safely out of a mouth with this trick but the target had to keep perfectly still. 'I'll do it,' said the chairman and bravely put a cigarette, unlit, into his mouth. Arthur positioned him just right to perform a trick he had done hundreds of times in he past. Just as Arthur flicked the yo-yo the train carriage swayed on the track and the yo-yo flicked the chairman's eyebrow rather than the ciggy. Arthur was most upset for the poor man who was quickly developing a black eye. It wasn't a serious injury but one that looked worse than it was. The chairman wasn't worried one bit but he did say to Arthur that his wife, who was at home, would think that he had been involved in a fight as she would never believe that he had received a black eye from Arthur Clues' yo-yo!

Ian Walsh the great Australian forward who toured England twice got to know Arthur well. In an interview in Australia he was asked if he had met Arthur on his tours over here. Ian replied: 'Yes, I know Arthur very well. He was a great Aussie forward who played a long time in England. He had a sports store in Leeds and was on the committee at the football club at Headingley. He would come across two or three times a week to see us at the Troutbeck Hotel at Ilkley where we stayed on tour. Arthur stood us many a meal in Leeds and advised us the best ways of beating the poms. Though he was married to a Leeds girl and had settled in the city permanently we all thought deep down that he was as Australian as ever. When he was out with us Aussie boys he would call the Englishmen, "Pommie Bastards". He was a great bloke, Arthur.'

When the Australian national airline, Qantas, opened its routes from Manchester to Sydney, the first flight had on board several invited guests, mostly Australian personalities from show business and sport. Arthur was one of those honoured guests.

Bill Carter who was secretary at Leeds RLFC for many years, taking over from George Hirst and serving the club until the early 1990s remembers Arthur with a tremendous respect. Bill rates Arthur as one of the most talented forwards ever to play for Australia and Leeds. His larger than life character had a truly huge impact on the game over here and Arthur became wonderfully memorable to all who met him or saw him play. Bill recalls that Arthur seemed to know everybody in this country. He could not go anywhere without being recognised. Bill reminds us that Arthur was responsible for the Leeds club signing many players who served Leeds proudly. Ken Thornett, the brilliant Australian full back, was one in particular who came over here on Arthur's recommendation totally unknown and returned to Australia to tour and indeed captain his country. But it was Arthur's charisma that nearly caused trouble for Bill and the Leeds' chief scout in South Wales. Leeds were trying secretly to sign the Welsh rugby union international scrum half, Colin Evans. Their intention was to meet Colin and bring him back the following morning to show him around Headingley and then discuss the terms of his contract before signing him.

Bill and Arthur met up with the Leeds scout in the Park Hotel in Cardiff. There was a big, swish do on at the Hotel that night (a dinner dance with a top comedian doing an act after the dinner and before the dancing). The signing of Welsh players by the Northern professional clubs was deemed sacrilege by the Welsh and lots of rugby union dignitaries attended this dance. Arthur, being Arthur, looked into the banqueting suite and was immediately spotted by the well known comedian, Ossie Morris, who was an old friend of Arthur. Ossie called over in a loud voice, 'Hello Cluesy, what are you doing down here boyo? On your holidays is it?'

Arthur replied equally as loud, 'Nah mate, we're down here to sign your best scrum half.'

Suddenly lots of shocked and angry faces turned towards Bill and Arthur. The scout was aghast and disappeared quickly as he was very well known around Cardiff and could not be openly associated with professional rugby league. When Bill and Arthur were safely in their room, Bill expressed both his and the scout's worry that word by now would be into the valleys and that the Welsh would move heaven and earth to stop the move. Arthur just smiled and said, 'Don't worry Bill, young Colin will sign for me,' and he did. Arthur could charm the birds from the trees.

Bill Carter also remembers Arthur travelling with the team to away games in his capacity as a football committee member. One game in particular, Wigan at Central Park, sticks in his mind. Wigan had amongst its great pack of forwards, Brian McTigue, the teak-tough international prop. Leeds had a local lad who had been transferred from near neighbours Bramley, Colin Tomlinson, himself a tough forward. Within minutes of the kick off McTigue and Tomlinson met head on in a fearsome collision. Brian McTigue groggily managed to stay upright, refusing to go down but Colin Tomlinson collapsed as if shot by a Lee-Enfield 303. Tomlinson was carted to the bench to be looked at by the physio and the club doctor, so fierce was the collision. Arthur was passing the bench on his way to his seat in the stand and he bobbed his head over the low wall. Just then Tomlinson was showing signs of coming back to earth but the clash had caused a slight concussion and some double vision. Arthur leaned a bit nearer and looked Tomlinson in the eye. 'How are you Colin mate?' Asked the brutally hard Clues.

'Okay I think,' said Tomlinson, 'but I can see two of him,' he said, pointing towards the nearest Wigan player.

Arthur looked at Tomlinson with an old fashioned look and the man who, when he played, hardly ever showed he was hurt said, 'Geez, that's no problem Colin. When you get back on just tackle both of 'em.'

Bill Carter considered Arthur to be an outstandingly durable and rugged player who could and would rough up the toughest opponent, was able to play skilful football with the best in the world and was an incredibly hard man on the field. Off the field, he was a big hearted, generous man with a colourful and out-going personality. Said Bill Carter, 'We may never see his like again.'

My personal memories of Arthur are of seeing him that evening at Headingley when he was 22 years old going out for his first training run. I remember admiring his football skills which I can categorically say were and still are the most unbelievably skilful and exciting that I ever saw in a forward and that includes all the talent I coached and players I played with or against in my many years in the game. But above all my memories are of an immense personality and strong character.

Arthur died on 3rd October 1998. He was 74 years old. The elderly gentleman who then struggled to walk because of severe arthritis in both knees was still the stuff of legends and I close by quoting the Australian author, Jack Pollard:

'He gave and took some fearful hidings but was never known to squawk and even in the partisan Yorkshire and Lancashire mill-towns they respected him for that. But for all his football wizardry on the field it is likely that Arthur Clues will be forever remembered for his salty, direct speech, which, through thousands of earthy footballers' post mortems, attracted to all men with red blood in their veins'.

APPENDIX 1

ARTHUR CLUES PLAYING RECORD IN AUSTRALIA

Western Suburbs RLFC

Debut v Balmain, away, 24 April 1943. Last Game v Canterbury Bankstown, home, 17 August 1946.

First Grade: 51 games.

Reserve Grade: 2 games.

Points (First Grade): 17 tries, 2 goals.

Representative Games

Australia: 3 games.

New South Wales: 7 games.

Rest Of NSW: 3 games.

City v Country: 3 games.

City Seconds: 1 game.

Metropolitan: 1 game.

Points: 4 tries.

Note: Arthur played in five extra games for Western Suburbs in cup ties in country centres which do not appear in Western Suburbs' club records.

APPENDIX 2

ARTHUR CLUES PLAYING RECORD IN ENGLAND

Leeds RLFC

Debut v Hull FC, home, 1 February 1947. Last Game v Dewsbury, home, 28 August 1954.

First Team: 238 games.

Points: 74 tries.

Hunslet RLFC

Debut v Bradford Northern, home, 9 October 1954. Last Game v Hull FC, away, 31 August 1957.

First Team: 83 games.

Points: 12 tries.

Representitive Games

Other Nationalities: 14 games.

The Rest v Great Britain Tourists at Wigan, 4 October 1950.

Australasia v Great Britain at Leeds, 19 May 1951.

British Empire v New Zealand at Chelsea AFC, 23 January 1952.

Rugby League XIII v Australasia at Bradford, 17 November 1954.

Rugby League XIII v Australia at Leigh, 29 October 1956.

Points (Other Nationalities): 2 tries.